You are about to discover . . .

- How an **unprecedented fearstorm** is rapidly sweeping across the human race . . .

- How **world developments** are following a script written before the foundatior of the world . . .

- How **six ancient predictions** have converged on our generation as never before in human history . . .

- What the prophets predicted about **human relationships** in Earth's final days . . .

- **Lucifer's "Master Strategy"** for our generation . . .

- How the stage is set for **increasing persecution** of those who love and obey God . . .

- **Ten practical strategies** for standing strong during the tough days ahead . . .

- How to be **effective parents** in today's increasingly hostile environment . . .

- God's promise of **ultimate victory** to those who follow His plan.

About the Author

In addition to serving as director of ministries for Trinity Evangelical Free Church in Redlands, California, **Larry W. Poland, Ph.D.** is founder and president of Mastermedia International, Inc., a ministry of spiritual support and guidance to leaders in the film and television industries. He meets regularly with Hollywood TV and movie executives, which has helped make him acutely aware of the forces for both good and evil that are at work in our nation's media.

Within the past two years, Poland has been interviewed on *Nightline, The MacNeil-Lehrer Newshour, Focus on the Family, Family News in Focus,* and on TV and radio talk shows in more than 25 of the country's major media markets.

He also appears daily on more than 110 radio stations (including Moody Radio Network) with his program, "The Mediator."

Larry W. Poland, Ph.D.

THE COMING PERSECUTION

Includes DISCUSSION GUIDE for Group Study

Here's Life Publishers

First Printing, January 1990
Second Printing, May 1990

Published by
HERE'S LIFE PUBLISHERS, INC.
P. O. Box 1576
San Bernardino, CA 92402

Library of Congress Cataloging-in-Publication Data
Poland, Larry W.
  How to prepare for the coming persecution / Larry Poland.
        p.   cm.
  ISBN 0-89840-277-8
  1. Persecution — United States — Miscellanea.   2. Christian life — 1960-
I. Title.
  BR1608.U6P65   1990
  272'.9 — dc 20   89-27767
  CIP

Cover illustration: R. DiCianni
Interior artwork: B. Bubnis

        Scripture quotations designated NIV are from *The Holy Bible: New International Version,* © 1973, 1978, 1984 by the International Bible Society. Used by permission of Zondervan Bible Publishers.
        Scripture quotations designated TLB are from *The Living Bible,* © 1971 by Tyndale House Publishers, Wheaton, Illinois.
        Scripture quotations designated NASB are from *The New American Standard Bible,* © The Lockman Foundation 1960, 1962, 1963, 1968, 1971, 1972, 1975, 1977.

For More Information, Write:
  L.I.F.E. — P.O. Box A399, Sydney South 2000, Australia
  Campus Crusade for Christ of Canada — Box 300, Vancouver, B.C., V6C 2X3, Canada
  Campus Crusade for Christ — Pearl Assurance House, 4 Temple Row, Birmingham, B2 5IIG, England
  Lay Institute for Evangelism — P.O. Box 8786, Auckland 3, New Zealand
  Campus Crusade for Christ — P.O. Box 240, Raffles City Post Office, Singapore 9117
  Great Commission Movement of Nigeria — P.O. Box 500, Jos, Plateau State Nigeria, West Africa
  Campus Crusade for Christ International — Arrowhead Springs, San Bernardino, CA 92414, U.S.A.

*To our children
who may have to endure more
of the coming persecution
than we.*

Contents

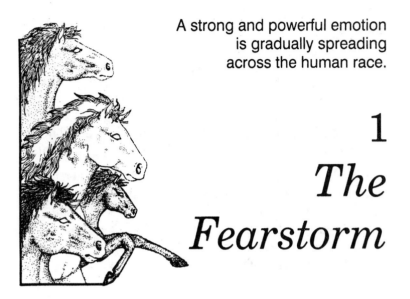

A strong and powerful emotion is gradually spreading across the human race.

1

The Fearstorm

"But mark this: there will be terrifying times in the last days."

Paul
2 Timothy 3:1

☐　　☐　　☐

It's a square knot somewhere in the abdomen, the jump-starting of the heartbeat, the rush of blood cells trampling over each other to get to the head, perspiration forming like dew in the palms and muscles quivering like guitar strings. When you experience it, the mind races in hyperspeed, concentration focuses into laser-like beams, the senses go on Red Alert and the mouth turns into the Sahara.

It is fear.

You know the feeling. So do I. Every member of our species has experienced it, and it's stunning how little it takes to trigger it.

A Fifty-Yard Mile

It was only a short walk to the car. The mall was nearly abandoned, and the closing-time exodus had left my buggy nearly alone in a remote corner of what, a few hours earlier, had been acres of vehicles in a giant parking lot.

Suddenly I froze. In that dark, far-off corner of the blacktop was a scuzzy-looking pickup truck. It was draped with a young band of toughs having their own version of a tailgate party on this late Saturday night. They looked really scary—headbands, earrings, dark eye sockets and other symbols of contempt for mainstream society.

What to do?

There was no turning back into the mall. The security men were already at the doors permitting exits but not entrances. None of the other handful of departing patrons seemed to be going my way to help me play a weak kind of strength-in-numbers game.

I breathed a quiet prayer for guidance, a second one for protection and, after a moment's hesitation, headed on.

As I got closer to my car, I calculated my moves so as to reduce even by milliseconds the time they consumed. The car key was in my hand, correctly positioned to slip quickly into the door. In my mind I practiced hitting the automatic door lock once I had closed the door.

Just a few more strides and I would be at the car.

Now they were looking at me. The guy with a week's growth of facial fuzz stared over the side-view mirror of the pickup at me as I drew closer. Two more who were plopped in the truck bed craned their necks my way as they heard my size-twelves slapping the pavement near them.

My heart was racing. I began to calculate what vehicular maneuver I might pull to shake them off if they attacked before I could get my car, which was grill-to-grill with their aging Ford, moving. If Indiana Jones and James Bond could escape their attackers in this way, it might work for a frightened Christian servant.

I was at my car. "Ziiippp-click" went the outside lock. "Brurrr-bam" went the door. "Snaap" went the automatic door lock switch. "Grrrr-a-grrrr-a-grrrr" complained the starter a moment before the engine roared.

A glance at the truck revealed that the youths had directed their attention back toward each other, continuing the fat-chewing they had begun long before this frightened man had invaded their turf.

I was safe.

Or was I?

Afraid I'm More Afraid

That night, as I reflected on the nearly half-century of my life, I wondered, *Why is this strange emotion of fear such an increasingly common experience?* I have never been thought of as a fearful person; *fearless* is a more common description. I don't think it can be assigned to aging or the loss of youthful naiveté which makes me more cautious. I certainly have never been diagnosed with even a smidgen of paranoia. More people have thought I was out to get them than I thought were out to get me.

Am I fearful because I am now part of an urban megalopolis, this kid from small-town, middle America? Is it because innocent adults have been murdered, little kids have been kidnapped and molested, and women have been raped in the community in which I live?

It certainly isn't because of weak faith in divine care — the kind of faith that drives out a "spirit of fear." Nor do I think my increasingly frequent fear feelings are the result of irrational and free-floating anxieties which bespeak some emotional instability.

What Franklin Delano Roosevelt said in a national crisis nearly five decades ago is wrong today. We *do* have something to fear besides fear. There are a lot more causes for legitimate fear today, and they are pressing closer to where you and I live.

I have another, call it "mystical," hypothesis. In the same way that dogs have been reported to have premonitions of their masters' deaths, and barnyard animals have been known to become restless before an earthquake, I believe the human race is getting an intuitive pre-warning of impending doom. I believe thinking people all over the planet are sensing, at the instinctive level, the storm building. They can smell the ozone in the air and sense the barometric pressure falling for the coming cataclysm.

But the real storm is being preceded by a hurricane of anxiety, a tornado of apprehension, a hailstorm of fright — a fearstorm.

The Facts Behind the Fears

I am not alone in this diagnosis. *New York Times* columnist Tom Wicker calls this the "Age of Apprehension," and gives several reasons why: There are possibilities of wars which could involve the two superpowers in at least seven regions of the world. There is continuing global fear of nuclear annihilation. The U. S. and the world are emerging slowly from the worst economic recession since the Great Depression, leaving the developing world in a debt crisis that could shake or shatter the world's financial order.[1]

Mention "October 19" to any American businessperson and he gets cold chills, even if he didn't lose tons of money in the stock market crash of 1987. Three years later, market analysts acknowledge that significant international skittishness still bedevils the investment world, fallout from that "Black Monday" blast which took stock markets in London, Tokyo and other global financial centers with it.

The rash of defaults by third world nations on loans to creditor nations, the shakiness of the American savings and loans, the near collapse of oil-based economies from the Middle East to Mexico to Houston, and the cosmic proportion of America's national debt are pushing up anxieties like fever pushes up a thermometer.

You and I aren't inoculated against this one, for these financial statistics are closely related to the trouble we may have making ends meet. If you give birth to a bouncing baby this year, the child will enter the world more than $50,000 in hock the first day of his life—his share of the U. S. national debt.[2] That debt is now past $2,000,000,000,000— two *trillion* dollars—and the government has to borrow more than half a *billion* dollars *every single day* just to pay the interest on the monster.[3] That means that someone is cutting little pieces out of all your dollar bills every minute that passes.

In addition to what Uncle Sam is trimming off our personal assets, we aren't doing badly at sending ourselves to the poorhouse. Consumer debt almost tripled during the decade 1977 to 1987, and 2.5 million American farmers borrowed more money than debt-plagued Mexico, Brazil and Argentina *combined*.[4] The average American carries such a heavy debt-load and has so little savings that he is threatened with economic disaster if he loses his income for six weeks.

If you are afraid you may be running out of money, you are.

We are also losing possessions at an unprecedented rate to people who apparently want them more than we do. Today I heard a radio ad for a heavy steel bar which locks on the steering wheel of your car to discourage thieves. In my pleasant neighborhood, some houses have bars over all the windows and doors. Virtually all of the homes have some kind of security system, some as simple as deadbolt locks and some as sophisticated as electronic systems which dial the police directly or include surveillance by armed patrolmen.

In 1988, theft in the U. S. amounted to a loss of $343 million, and the probability of someone breaking into our houses to steal some of our earthly goods is one out of four this year. If this is *your* year to get hit, you can count on more trauma than just the loss of goods. The FBI report notes:

> The impact of this violent crime on its victims cannot be measured in terms of monetary loss alone. While the object of a robbery is to obtain money or property, the crime always involves force or the threat of force, and many victims suffer serious, personal injury.[5]

From Contamination to Child Care

Then there is the AIDS fear. Hostesses serve paper plates to known homosexuals for fear of having the lethal virus reach their kitchens. Parents pull their children out of school because of a single student who got AIDS from a blood transfusion. Fearful and angry that Louise and Clifford Ray planned to send their three AIDS-infected children to school, residents of Arcadia, Florida, burned the Rays' home to the ground.[6]

Family members line up to give blood for ailing friends and relatives to avoid the risk of having a loved one get the disease that is both 100 percent incurable and 100 percent fatal.

That is called fear—F-E-A-R.

Then there are our precious kids. Think back, if you are a parent, to the relative freedom from fear your parents exhibited in raising you. Now compare it to the precautions you and other parents exercise today. Would you, for a minute, allow your child the freedom to roam the streets and neighborhoods of your town like your parents permitted you to do? I doubt it.

And why? The sexual revolution took place since you were born.

This "revolution" means there are hundreds of thousands of morally sick people across this land seeking to prey on our children. There are hundreds of *child* pornography magazines being distributed across the nation and read by people who fantasize about sexual acts with little boys and girls like ours.

Father Bruce Ritter, founder of the Covenant House in New York City, knows about the sexual revolution. He invests a lot of his time trying to piece together the shattered lives of kids who have been brutalized at the hands of pornographers and pimps. In his book, *God Has a Kid's Face*, he tells a story about a little girl who had been arrested eight times for prostitution and was thrown out of a window to her death by her pimp—all before her twelfth birthday. Then there was the ten-year-old boy who wandered into Covenant House bearing the toy cars and trucks adult "customers" had given in exchange for sex acts.

Father Ritter says, "Just once, try to look at a picture of a three-year-old in a sex act with an animal while an adult takes her photograph."[7]

Hustler magazine has run a cartoon feature for thirteen years which portrays a lecherous Chester the Molester lusting after young girls and often having sexual encounters with them. The cartoonist who draws the twisted character, forty-three-year-old Dwaine Tinsley, was himself arrested on nine charges of sexual molestation including charges involving a girl under the age of fourteen.[8] Who knows how many secret "Chesters" there are out there waiting to scar our daughters for life to fulfill their twisted sexual urges? Not far from our home a minister at an evangelical Christian church was caught molesting the kids at the church's preschool.

Despite what the gay rights people would like to have you believe about the acceptability of their lifestyle, the homosexual way of life commonly involves "cruising" or some other form of search for young, fresh sexual partners. During the course of one research study on AIDS, it was discovered the average homosexual interviewed had had 550 sexual partners. The AIDS victims averaged 1,100 different sexual partners with some reporting as many as 20,000.[9] This means that every day sexually addicted homosexuals in communities across America are out looking for attractive young men and boys whom they can introduce to the world of sodomy and oral sex.

No wonder parents now keep a fearfully close eye on their precious young sons and daughters while out shopping, at the county fair or other public functions. Can you honestly say that the threat of sexual molestation hasn't occurred to you even when hiring a new babysitter or dropping your child off at a child care facility?

The Day the Gangs Took Over Our Country

Consider the drug/gang crisis. As you read this, more than a dozen drug/gang networks are spreading out of the highly policed, urban areas of the U. S. and opening up "new territories" for drug traffic in small, rural towns across America. Out-manned, out-gunned and intimidated, police and sheriff's departments in hundreds of medium-sized and small cities now realize they have lost control of their own communities to a ruthless, well-financed, heavily armed, international band of terrorists.

In its most exaggerated form, the drug/gang crisis turns neighborhoods into war zones of death and destruction. Residents of the Red Hook housing project in South Brooklyn, New York, fall into three categories: dealers, users or hostages to the drug trade. Crack, the powerful cocaine derivative sold at five dollars a hit, has turned the Red Hook development into a Vietnam of violent crime. Even non-users live in constant fear. Many will not leave their own apartments lest they stumble onto a hallway drug deal and get shot. Some families carry a can of mace with them when they take out the trash. Others let the trash pile up until they can go to the dumpsters in groups. One Red Hook resident said, "We don't know from one day to the next if we will make it to work or home."[10]

This torment is not limited to inner city housing developments. A friend of mine pulled his expensive, late model car into a parking garage in fashionable Westwood, California, not far from Beverly Hills. Two gang members accosted him, cursed him and emptied the contents of a handgun into his chest. Investigation later revealed that the assailants were members of a gang in which the rite of initiation is to "off a honky." But for the grace of God my friend would be dead.

You know we are in trouble when the federal government seriously considers using the military or the National Guard to help fight the drug/gang war. You know things are out of control when the Los Angeles police department repeatedly puts *one thousand* additional officers on the streets on random sweeps in an effort to stop the drug dealing, gang slaughter and drive-by shootings — only to have the effort fail.

And When You Put It All Together...

My dear friend, this combination of fear factors is unprecedented in the history of the world.

Due to high-tech firepower, high-speed transportation and delivery systems, and international cartels of organized criminals, the drug/gang crisis is exponentially worse than China's opium wars or the rum running of the Prohibition era.

The global AIDS crisis has greater potential for human destruction than the black plague, yellow fever, polio and small pox epidemics rolled into one.

The international spread of pornographic films, videos, tele-porn, computer porn and hard-core literature is feeding the insatiable global lust for perverse and uncontrolled sexual pursuits. In America today there are more adult bookstores than there are McDonald's restaurants and the global porn trade is estimated in the hundreds of billions of dollars.[11] I saw an American porn magazine for sale in a store in Nazareth, Israel, the childhood home town of Jesus Christ!

The satellite-computer linkup of the world's banking, investing and financial structures creates an unprecedented potential for total, global depression triggered in an instant. By one scenario, this could be triggered by a catastrophic earthquake in Tokyo, now the financial capital of planet Earth. When Tokyo itches, Wall Street scratches. If Tokyo gets cardiac arrest, what will keep Wall Street from dying?

As the World Turns

Beyond all this, there looms a spectre even more insidious than anything I've yet described. We've seen it in the past, and we're going to see it again. In many circles, it's already begun.

Persecution. The deliberate, calculated terrorizing of a group of people because of their religious beliefs, political viewpoints or national/ethnic heritage.

In a world sprinkled with thousands of examples of hideous inhumanity to inhumanity, we must ask ourselves, "Could they turn on *me*?" How can we understand the superterror of being hunted like an animal, being branded The Traitor, The Enemy, The Problem. What must it be like to have to hide like rats in cellars and crawl spaces? What words can express the horror of being branded, tattooed, head-shaved, marked for extermination? What groaning of the human spirit can articulate the receipt of the raucous ridicule, the demeaning derision, the awful abuse and terrible torture of hate-fueled masses?

Lest we take comfort in the protection of the great American system of free press, let me remind you that never in the history of a civilization has a single cadre of individuals *who do not share the dominant values of their society* wielded so much power to shape and alter the thinking of the masses. With the average American home glued to the tube seven-and-a-half to nine hours *every single day,* the media elite are more powerful in creating and twisting public opinion than the government. So great is this power that elected officials themselves live in more fear of the media's cameras and microphones than they do an assassin's bullet. Murder by media is far more commonplace.

Before you are through with this book, we will have documented for you the turning of the media elite against values you hold dear. You will see the fangs of the secular press reaching out to claw to pieces any rivals to its hedonistic, relativistic, man-centered world view.

Why, you ask, *have you spent all of this time sharing this horrific stuff with me? I didn't pick up this book to be depressed by volumes of gloom and doom! I can get that on the six o'clock news.*

Glad you asked. I have a method to this non-madness.

You see, I am out to convince you that none of this is happening by chance, that it was all predicted by a school of prophets in the first century A.D., and that world developments are following the lines of a script written before the foundations of the world by the only one who writes history *before* it happens.

I want to show you that the global fear I have described here is just the first of a set of distinguishing benchmarks ancient seers set forth to identify the end of human civilization as we know it.

Before your reading is over — if you'll stick with me — you'll . . .

- Explore a number of other incontrovertible proofs of the perfect accuracy of these first-century prophetic voices.
- Peer into the coming decades and see how these devastating dynamics are carried to their logical and, I believe, divinely predetermined conclusions.

- Learn the effect all of this is having on the collective core of human character.

- Discover what group of people become the global scapegoats in these worldly upheavals and how they become universally hated and persecuted. (Could you be in that group?)

- Study a strategy for coping with the international trauma now in its beginning stages.

- Receive practical hints for managing your family and parenting your kids in an increasingly hostile environment.

- Find out how the whole cataclysmic upheaval ends—either in a hideous megacaust of human agony or in a glorious and enrapturing cosmic finale of human deliverance.

For now, reflect on the stages of progressive fearfulness that have slipped silently upon you. But don't be surprised by them. First-century prophets said this would happen to you.

One, writing under the influence of the divine Spirit in about A.D. 63, said, "But mark this: there will be terrifying times in the last days."[12]

Another, Jesus of Nazareth, in answering a question about signs of the end of the world, declared, "Men will faint from terror, apprehensive of what is coming on the world . . . "[13]

So, reign in your fear and read on, friend. But don't get so involved in digesting the morsels of this chapter that you fail to watch out on the way to your car.

You may not make it to Chapter 2.

The public's respect for Christians is rapidly changing.
And not necessarily for the better.

2

Twenty (Loaded) Questions

"Everyone who wants to live a godly life will be persecuted..."

Paul
2 Timothy 3:12

☐   ☐   ☐

It was all backwards.

I was on the telephone with the president of a major state university. He was seeking my counsel because he learned of my involvement at the heart of the Christian response to Universal Pictures' movie release, *The Last Temptation of Christ.*

He explained his dilemma. More than a year after the movie's release, the student government at his university had requested a showing of *Last Temptation* on campus.

The administration had not granted approval. A tremendous controversy arose with the administration standing accused of censorship. The board of regents concurred with the administration's decision. Ministers in the community where the university is located supported the administration about fifty to one. The hundreds of letters that poured in were running ten to one in favor of the administration as well.

But what really prompted the president's call was that the university — president, regents, *et al.* — had been sued in an effort to get the courts to force the showing of the film. And the suit was filed by the American Civil Liberties Union!

Let me explain why the ACLU's action is so absolutely incredible by asking a few questions. Who is it who goes into cardiac arrest every time the smell of religion is detected in public life? Who has engaged in legal terrorism against virtually every type of public institution to remove every hint of religion out of tax-supported America? Who gets dyspeptic every time a public school has a prayer in its ceremonies? Who litigates to get religious activities and groups banned from state university facilities and campuses? Who seeks to get all religious Christmas observances out of public education and manger scenes off the courthouse lawns of America?

You know the answer.

The ACLU.

But now it is suing a state university to force it to show a *religious movie on campus.* It is trying to get the court to compel a board of regents to back down on a decision *not* to show a film about Jesus Christ. It is demanding that the university permit the showing of a film that its director, Martin Scorsese, calls a "deeply religious film," a film based on a novel by a man who declared he wanted his writings to be the basis for a new religion.

What caused the ACLU flip-flop? Could it be because *this* religious film is an *attack* on Christianity? Could it be because *this* religious film maligns the founder of the Christian faith? Could it be because Christians don't want the film shown?

Okay, accuse me of paranoia. One of my favorite posters declares, *Just Because You Aren't Paranoid Doesn't Mean Everybody Isn't Out to Get You!* And one of my favorite Gary Larson cartoons shows two deer in the forest, one with a perfect target and bullseye on his chest. The other deer says to him, "Bummer of a birthmark, Hal."

Could it be that things are turning against Christians on a global scale? We will devote a significant part of this book to answering that question. We'll explore whether a time is nearing when—even if we aren't paranoid—everybody will be out to obliterate the human rights of those who believe in Jesus Christ. We will examine whether the time draws near when every Christian will, in essence, bear a "bummer of a birthmark."

For now, let me leave you with . . .

Twenty (Loaded) Questions

Yes   No

____   ____   1. Does it seem to you that the media seldom, if ever, give the Christian lifestyle a fair presentation?

____   ____   2. Can you think of any primetime TV series cast in a contemporary setting in which Christians are prominent and are treated with authenticity, respect and compassion?

___   ___   3. Have you noted unusual viciousness in the press treatment of televangelists who have fallen, viciousness not equally meted out to fallen politicians, athletes or representatives of other religious groups?

___   ___   4. Have you felt that police and press treatment of Operation Rescue's pro-life protesters has been in keeping with the protesters' passive, non-violent methods and quiet-spirited approach?

___   ___   5. Do you feel that the use of the RICO anti-racketeering laws to convict pro-life protesters and slap them with *triple damages* is fair and consistent with actions taken against protesters in other causes like anti-nuclear, gay and lesbian, and environmental movements?

___   ___   6. Do you feel that contempt for Christians is mounting in public education because Christians have fought sex education curricula featuring "safe sex" techniques, "values clarification" classes, school-based health clinics and obscenity in school libraries?

___   ___   7. Do you sense the "academic freedom" of American colleges and universities is skewed so there is more freedom to speak as an anarchist, Marxist, Satanist, gay or lesbian, than there is to speak as a "born again" Christian, a creationist or a pro-life advocate?

__ __ 8. Do you feel the media have singled out Christians for contempt because of their persistent denunciation of gay and lesbian lifestyles and sexual practices?

__ __ 9. Do you think TV and movie productions portray Christians in the same favorable manner as they do Jews, Muslims, blacks, native Americans, Hispanics, gays, lesbians and other groups?

__ __ 10. Do you sense words like *evangelical, fundamentalist* and *born-again Christian* have become "negatively charged" in the way they are used in public life today?

__ __ 11. Do you sometimes feel that the cherished family values you hold, like the sanctity of marriage, chastity before marriage, marital fidelity, the destructive nature of divorce, are no longer held by the society around you, and that you are now in an unappreciated minority?

__ __ 12. Do you feel more reluctant today to let it be known that you are a Christian than you used to?

__ __ 13. Do you feel that your commitment to truthfulness, honesty and integrity increasingly puts you at odds with those around you?

___ ___ 14. Do you feel that a major American film studio would have released a movie defaming a religious leader of another faith or a leader of another racial, ethnic or religious subgroup as Universal Pictures did in 1988 by releasing *The Last Temptation of Christ*?

___ ___ 15. Do you feel that the society around you does not appreciate a belief in the existence of absolute moral standards and the reality of such a concept as "sin"?

___ ___ 16. Do you feel that any opposition to nudity, explicit sex, violence, profanity and anti-Christian content in the media is viewed by others as puritanical or "censorship"?

___ ___ 17. Have you detected an increasing mistrust of and contempt for the institutional church and even a desire to undermine it by every means, from denial of its income tax exemption to efforts to compromise or discredit its leadership?

___ ___ 18. Have you perceived an increase in occult activity such as horoscopes, channeling, incantations and Satan worship, and felt that perhaps it explains in part the increase of crimes against churches, Christian believers and Christian organizations?

___ ___ 19. Do you feel there is a developing youth subculture which is assaulting traditional moral and spiritual values and turning the young against Judeo-Christian value structures and moral norms?

___ ___ 20. Have you observed more and more responsible spiritual leaders proclaiming apocalyptic messages of end-time tribulation and persecution?

What if your answer to any or all of these is "Yes"? Is there any way you can know where all of this is heading and, if a battle is heating up, whether there is a way to fight and *win* the battle?

There is.

You came to the right place.

Climb aboard for a journey that will take you on a 2000-year voyage into the *known*. Beginning with a handful of humble prophets in the first century and ending with a view of the end of the world, your passage will take you right through the middle of the late twentieth century — right where you live and work.

Keep alert at every stage of the trip. Watch carefully what is happening all around you. Keep your hands and arms inside the train. And don't be surprised if, when the journey is over, you discover that you and your loved ones can stand strong in the face of trial, find hope in a hopeless world and look forward to a brighter future.

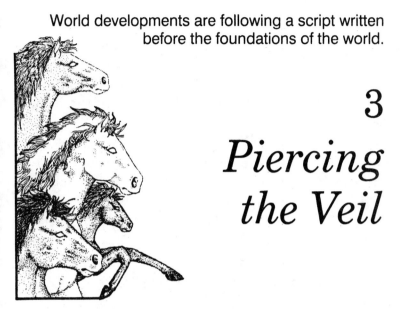

World developments are following a script written before the foundations of the world.

3

Piercing the Veil

"See, I have told you ahead of time."

Jesus Christ
Matthew 24:25

☐   ☐   ☐

It's tough, isn't it, deciding if anyone, anywhere can see into the future and foretell it? I can appreciate your skepticism. I am sure most of mine would still be intact if it were not for a continuing series of experiences like one I had south of the equator.

Colombian High

Ernesto and I were obviously enjoying each other. Providence and some Colombian airline ground personnel had stuck us next to each other on the flight from Cali to Bogota, and neither of us was complaining about the placement.

Ernesto was an American-born Hispanic but had lived and worked in South America for years for a division of the United Nations. He seemed eager to (a) talk to an American, (b) talk English, (c) talk to someone who enjoyed a good laugh.

I was enjoying the unfolding of his life story from the American Southwest to the circuit-riding role he played for the U.N. He possessed that Latin warmth, joviality and passion that I love and his eyes revealed a high mischief quotient that seemed, at least partly, to be restrained by his maturity and master's degree.

The shifting hum of the engines and the accompanying chime and seat belt light cued us that we were entering our descent in the Bogota area. Both Ernesto and I were surprised the time had passed so quickly and implicitly acknowledged that the good company was the primary reason for the rapid passage.

We exchanged business cards, said warm goodbyes and filed cattle-like off the plane and to the baggage area.

I suppose you are figuring this to be another acquaintanceship swallowed in the quicksands of time and distance, no? No.

I watched the taxi driver wrest Ernesto's luggage from him and wondered if I would ever see him again. That question must have triggered some response in the heavens, because a thought arrived at my frontal lobe as if placed there by some cosmic speaker: *Larry, you didn't share your faith with Ernesto.*

The thought-words stung as I realized I had not. There was no excuse for me not to have shared the most significant dimension of my life with my new friend. I had had plenty of time. We had enjoyed a wonderful rapport, the kind of rapport which leads people to share things they probably wouldn't tell their doctors. Guilty as charged.

I'm sorry, Lord, I responded, with thought-words of my own. *Forgive me. I should have expressed my faith to him. I trust You will get the message to him somehow.* As a sort of afterthought I added, *If You want to use me, I'm available.*

The next few days were airline hops and visits to Lima, Peru, and spots around the eastern coast of the continent followed by an inland foray to Bolivia—La Paz and Santa Cruz. Nearly two weeks after meeting Ernesto, I was scheduled for a Thursday flight from Santa Cruz to Sao Paulo, Brazil.

But every seasoned traveler will tell you that third world airline schedules aren't worth the disappearing ink used to print them. Flights have a way of moving mysteriously around the schedule, changing aircraft, making unscheduled stops, bumping you for some dignitary or just "plane vanishing" into thin air.

The Thursday Sao Paulo flight from Santa Cruz did just that—it vanished. And you can be assured that there was no catching the next flight in two hours. The next flight was two *days* away—if it didn't vanish as well.

Saturday seemed strangely like *déjà vu*: same airport, same airline, same departure time, same destination, same uncertainty as to whether this one would fly. It did.

Campo Grande, Señor

Vast Brazilian farmlands, mile after mile of campos inhabited by neither man nor livestock passed beneath the craft. This was a non-stop to Sao Paulo. At least the schedule said it was non-stop. So you can imagine my surprise when the engine power dropped, the seat belt light lit up and the pilot announced we were landing in Campo Grande, Brazil.

Grief! The sky was crystal clear and I should have seen a city, a town, a building—anything. But there was nothing there, only ranch land. The plane rapidly lost altitude, and the pilot entered what obviously was his final approach.

We could have been landing in the lost city of Atlantis for all I could see. But, wait, there was a building about the size of a large double garage at the end of a dirt road. The plane touched down on a grassy landing strip and taxied to the double garage which, indeed, bore the inscription "Campo Grande."

A half-dozen people stood in line alongside a wagon piled with a few pieces of baggage pulled by a human beast of burden.

It was great fun taking in the entire scene of the Campo Grande International Airport where passengers were now beginning to board—an Indian woman, a businessman, a—wait! That guy surely does look familiar. Ernesto!

When Ernesto boarded, I stood up and waved him to the rear of the aircraft to an empty seat next to mine. We shared shocked greetings and then buckled in.

"Larry," Ernesto said cautiously, "This is strange."

"Why?" I asked.

"Because of what happened back in Bogota."

"What happened?" Ernesto had me on the run.

"When I was leaving the airport after our flight

together, it was as if a voice said to me, 'You will see this man again. He has a message to which you must listen.'"

"Ernesto," I jumped in excitedly, "I have only one message worth listening to . . . " And I shared the wonderful joy of having a personal relationship with God through Jesus Christ.

Ernesto listened. Did he *ever* listen!

Take a Hike, Lady Luck

How did this happen?

- The "voice" I heard rebuking me for not sharing my religious faith on the first flight.
- The "voice" Ernesto heard assuring him he would see me again and that I had a critical message for him.
- The "chance" of meeting many days and many countries later.
- The "cancellation" of Thursday's flight from Santa Cruz.
- The "unscheduled stop" in Campo Grande, hardly the hub of planet Earth.

If you say "coincidence," I'll recommend a psychiatrist! The exponents needed to quantify these odds are astronomical. After all,

Somebody had to *know* . . .

Somebody had to *know* before it happened.

Somebody had to *know before* as well as *during* the events.

Somebody had to *intervene, guide, control* . . .

Somebody who could *see ahead*.

This could be treated as a rare, stranger-than-fiction occurrence if it were not for some striking realities. First, this kind of experience, this reception of extrasensory information and guidance, is an increasingly common occurrence in my life. Second, this kind of experience is commonly reported in the lives of Christian believers all over the world today and for the last two thousand years. And third, the Holy Scriptures declare both that God reveals His innermost secrets to those who are His own and that "those who are led by the Spirit of God are the sons of God."[1]

Finally, a Prophet You Can Trust

You see, even though I reject flatly the supermarket tabloid prognosticators and the "low percentage seers" like Nostradamus and Jeanne Dixon, I cannot reject the evidence supporting the reliability of the biblical prophets.

Why? First, no body of prophetic voices in history has faced tighter policing for accuracy. The rule established by the God of Moses Himself was that if a prophet presented himself as speaking for God and had even *one prophecy* that didn't come true, the prophet was to be declared a false prophet and become history himself—killed![2]

Second, no body of prophets has created such an immense volume of predictive prophecy only to have it found faultless over a span of nearly 3500 years. Approximately 40 percent of Scripture was predictive prophecy when it was written, and approximately four-fifths of that prophecy has been fulfilled—just as it said it would be. This provides a rather substantial test base for evaluating the accuracy of biblical prophecy on empirical grounds.

Third, I know of no other collection of prophets who

(1) wrote over a period of 1400 years, (2) wrote from different cultural, historical and linguistic backgrounds, (3) for the most part, never met each other nor had access to common literature from which to draw their prophetic pronouncements, and (4) came up with precisely the same conclusions regarding such potentially abstract or divisive topics as the nature of God, the nature of man, the way of spiritual salvation and the scheme of future world events.

Over 300 prophecies were fulfilled in the person and ministry of Jesus Christ Himself, prophecies written, for the most part, 250 years before He appeared on the world scene and fulfilled the prophecies. Furthermore, the fulfillment was marked by incredible precision even though the prophecies went far beyond Christ's ability to control their fulfillment. Examples are the time, place and manner of His birth, the manner of His betrayal—right down to the fact that *thirty* pieces of silver would be paid for it (not twenty-nine or thirty-one)—and the nature of His piercing and death.[3]

On this basis I listen more carefully when biblical prophets speak than E. F. Hutton would have us believe people listen to their financial advice.

From Ancient Seers to Current Events

Why, you ask, *are you building this case for biblical prophecy?*

Because the remaining "unfulfilled fifth" of biblical prophecy is rapidly being converted into current events here at the end of the second millennium A.D. That fifth describes events which are appearing in each day's newspaper—dynamics you're dealing with on a daily basis—and a "sprint to the finish" for this age with some predictions which aren't pretty.

There is tremendous benefit in knowing the future — whether it's knowing Ed McMahon is going to present you with a million dollar sweepstakes check or knowing your house is going to burn to the ground. Knowing the future would be absolutely indispensable if you could know whether you were headed for persecution or prosperity. If the future weren't important to you, you wouldn't have purchased insurance, be chipping in to a retirement plan, be getting stock market projections from your broker or following weather forecasts.

It is inconceivable to me that we would ignore the famous last words of the biblical prophets who tell us in detail what is going to happen at the end of the age. In a world where readers of mystery novels often race to the last chapter to find out if "the butler did it," how can we ignore the book of the Revelation? Revelation is largely unfulfilled prophecy and contains references so precisely geared to our generation (more so than all others) that it is spooky.

Just two examples should make the point. Critics of Revelation in the past have had a great time scoffing at two predictions in the book. One is the "wild and ridiculous" notion that any world ruler could so control commerce that he could enforce a ban on all buying or selling for a selected group of people who refused to take his official mark. But that is the unmistakable prediction made of the antichrist by the prophet John:

> He also forced everyone, small and great, rich and poor, free and slave, to receive a mark on his right hand or on his forehead, so that no one could buy or sell unless he had the mark, which is the name of the beast [the antichrist] or the number of his name.[4]

Stand Right in Front of the Laser Beam

Think how utterly incredible this concept would have been in any previous generation, including that of our parents and the early years of our own lives. Why, to keep people from buying or selling *anything*, one would have to have a system of finance so completely unified in its processes and so completely tied to cashless transactions that it would render all financial dealings outside the system null and void.

You're smiling. You must have tried to rent a car with cash. You must have tried to do business with a bank, a securities broker or the government without giving your social security number. You must have gotten a message from the IRS that you failed to report an item their computer coughed up from a 1099 document you overlooked. You must have stood helplessly and endlessly in line with other computer-age refugees at a major store because their computers were down. You must have found yourself blushing in the front of a checkout line—unable to buy or sell—because some mysterious little machine told the cashier the "mark" of your credit card was not acceptable.

My bank manager friend with Bank of America tells me that all their managers have been briefed on the advent of totally cashless economics—societies in which all financial transactions are electronic transfers by computer. He tells me their briefings included reference to the mega-computer in Belgium that will tie all world finance together. They call it—get this—The Beast.

Name one previous generation in the thousands of years of human history in which this prophecy could have taken place. The scoffers of this prophetic "absurdity" are looking rather silly themselves these days.

Tea for Two and Two for TV

Critics of biblical prophecy have also belly-laughed over the utter lunacy of a statement made by John in the eleventh chapter of his revelation. In that chapter John tells about the advent of two divinely empowered prophetic witnesses who will come to the earth proclaiming the message of the living God for 1260 days before they meet their comeuppance in Jerusalem at the hands of the antichrist.

John describes the scene after their murder:

> Their bodies will lie in the street of the great city... where also their Lord was crucified. For three and a half days men from every people, tribe, language, and nation *will gaze on their bodies* and refuse them burial [emphasis added].[5]

"Now you tell me," was the scoffers' challenge, "how a sampling of *all the peoples of the world* will be able to *see* the bodies of these two men lying in the streets of Jerusalem?"

This doesn't cause you any wonderment, does it, you child of the twenty-first century? You sit through the evening news with *live* scenes from all over the world via satellite. Why, you saw live action on the moon, on Mars, on Saturn and on Jupiter! What's the big deal about seeing two guys lying dead on the streets of Jerusalem? You've probably *already* seen dead guys on Jerusalem's streets. This prediction is pretty ho-hum stuff to you. But mind the fact that this is the first quarter century in the millennia of man in which such a happening has even been considered remotely possible, much less ho-hum.

And, as for a sampling of all the world's people witnessing the prophetic event, more than a third of the world's people saw or heard part of the last international

Olympic events from Seoul, Korea. It doesn't stretch my imagination any to have the peoples of the world watching events in Jerusalem if they already have watched events in Seoul.

The Whistle Just Blew for the Fifth Quarter

Are you getting the point? Here at the end of the century that is turning the corner into the twenty-first one since Christ and the fiftieth or sixtieth one since Eden, there is a convergence of dynamics which, *for the first time ever,* has prepared the world for the fulfillment of the final fifth of God's revealed scenarios. The "melting of the earth with a fervent heat" is now possible due to nuclear power man had unleashed *only fifty years ago.* Spectacular "signs in the heavens" are now possible in a space age which was ushered in only slightly more than *thirty years ago* and now includes shuttles in and out of earth orbits, space stations and "star wars" defense systems with particle beam weapons.

Friend, you are living in the beginning of the end. No longer is the so-called "prophet of doom" a bearded, white-robed kook carrying a sandwich board reading, "Repent! The end of the world is near!" The prophets of doom are on the six o'clock news. Even the august Club of Rome, a distinguished bevy of intellectuals gathered to postulate the future of humanity, determined that there are a dozen challenges facing mankind which could undo the race in this century. They concluded that these problems are so overwhelming in their magnitude that man will not only be unable to solve them, he will not even come fully to understand them.

And in the midst of this global panic, a divine voice whispers in Ernesto's and Larry's ears, guides them over a continent, readjusts their flight schedules and creates a "divine appointment" in a two-bit farm community on the back side of Brazil. He can do this. He *knows the future.* He reveals it. He shapes it. He rules it. Therefore, He can predict it.

God's vision pierces the veil which hides the future from us.

He whispered in the ears of a junta of men in the Middle East in the first century. He told them what would happen in the last century. Now He guides the affairs of men and nations like a grand master at the chess board. He is readjusting human events to fit His schedule. He is creating a "divine appointment" most of humanity isn't going to enjoy. He can do this. He *knows the future.* He reveals it. He shapes it. He rules it. He has predicted it.

Just what does the future hold . . . and . . . should we go to work Monday?

How five ancient predictions have converged on our generation as never before in human history.

4

Labor Pains

"Watch out that no one deceives you. For many will come in my name, claiming, 'I am the Christ,' and will deceive many. You will hear of wars and rumors of wars, but see to it that you are not alarmed. Such things must happen, but the end is still to come. Nation will rise against nation, and kingdom against kingdom. There will be famines and earthquakes in various places. All these are the beginning of birth pains."

Jesus
Matthew 24:4-8

☐   ☐   ☐

You're an obstetrician.

You've been seeing Mrs. Gulliver for about seven months now. She came to you experiencing some unusual physical symptoms. She had been feeling nauseated and had some vomiting. She was experiencing tenderness in her breasts and tiring easily. Her monthly cycle was completely off-track. She couldn't figure out what was wrong.

You didn't have any trouble figuring it out. You had the joy of announcing that little feet would soon be pitter-pattering around the Gulliver household. Mrs. G was about eight weeks into the process of creating a new living being.

From that first visit you knew what could be expected—you've read the books. You knew Mrs. Gulliver would continue to get larger in the abdomen. You knew in the fourth or fifth month she would feel some movement in her womb for the first time and, about that same time, you would be able to put the stethoscope to her abdomen and hear a tiny heartbeat. You also knew about some of the less exciting dimensions of the process—the backaches, the leg cramps, the swelling of the feet and ankles.

You knew even more discomfort awaited her in just ten days if she were to go full term.

The phone's for you. It's Mrs. Gulliver.

"Doctor," she complains anxiously, "I don't know what could be wrong. I have a kind of tightness in my thighs. The aching I have been having in my lower back is getting much more intense. It starts at the back and radiates around to the front. In fact, it seems as if the pains are coming in waves a few minutes apart. Also, I have this really strange sensation in my emotions that I can't explain. I'm really miserable. What do you think it could be?"

Incredulous that an intelligent woman like this one can't figure out what is happening, you reply, "It's time for you to deliver, Mrs. Gulliver."

"Oh, no, Doctor. That can't be it. You see, I've been feeling great! I've been taking my vitamins, getting lots of rest and exercising like you said. I have been in wonderful health until these strange pains and other symptoms started just a couple of hours ago."

"Mrs. Gulliver, this is all normal. I told you all of these things would happen. You are a week or so earlier than we had estimated, but trust me. I know what I'm talking about."

"Well, I'm sorry, Doctor, but I just can't accept this. I'm going to have to call another doctor for a second opinion. You see, my husband and I are catching a flight to Rio this afternoon. We have been planning this time away for two years. I won't let your phony childbirth notions interfere with my plans." Click.

How stupid of Mrs. Gulliver to ignore your predictions, to deny the tell-tale signs of the impending delivery and to pretend that those waves of back pain would somehow go away. You know that your diagnosis is accurate. You've read the books!

Pregnant Prophecies

I find it intriguing that in the most expansive, prophetic vision of the end of the age given by Jesus, He likened the first signs of the end time to "the beginning of birth pains."[1] The question from His disciples could not have been more direct: "When will these things be and what will be the sign of your own visible return and the complete finish of the eon?" Jesus laid out the identifying marks of the end of the age in two stages — the *beginnings* of birth pains and the *actual labor*.

Putting the prophecies of Jesus together with the prophecies of three others — Jude, Peter and Paul — we see that the *beginnings* of the birth pains are:

1. A significant and widespread increase in famines.

2. A significant and widespread increase in earthquakes.

3. A dramatic increase in the number of phony "messiahs."

4. A radical increase in national and ethnic wars and war rumors.

5. A predominance of intellectual and religious scoffers who ridicule the notion of the waning era of man or of any impending catastrophe.

6. A radical degeneration in the collective character of man.[2]

Not unlike Mrs. Gulliver's "strange" symptoms, these six *beginnings* signify that actual "labor" cannot be far away. If these prophecies are indeed true, then we are witnessing the beginning of the end of the earth as we know it.

1. The Famine Phantasmagoria

When I was a kid, we studied the theories of a man named Thomas Robert Malthus, an English economist at the turn of the eighteenth century. Malthus argued from raw mathematical principles that population growth, since it was exponential, would inevitably outstrip agricultural production, making it impossible to feed the world's people.

For most of the century-and-a-half after Malthus's famous 1798 "Essay on the Principle of Population," it was generally conceded by the academic community that Malthus not only was dead, but he was dead wrong. Tremendous breakthroughs in irrigation techniques, powerful chemical fertilizers and high-tech methods of agricultural production made it appear there was no end to our ability to stay ahead of the numbers in feeding the world's people.

Nobody ridicules Malthus now. After thousands of years of human history, the last 120 years have witnessed the most devastating famines in the age of man. In the 1870s a famine swept the Deccan plateau of southern India, killing five million people. In that same period, a famine in China killed nine million. In the late 1960s and 1970s, lack of rain produced widespread famine in a region of Africa called the Sahel. This brought starvation to parts of Senegal, Mauritania, Mali, Burkina Faso, Niger, Nigeria, Chad and the Sudan. In that same time period, famine struck parts of Kenya, Somalia and Ethiopia.[3]

Famine struck Africa again in the 1980s. The Ethiopian part of that famine was catastrophic. Since the late sixties, millions upon millions of Africans have died of hunger or hunger-related causes.

But not all famine is a function of drought or natural disaster: Famine has become a military strategy in many parts of the world. In the Nigerian civil war in 1967-70, armies deliberately created a famine to starve their enemies into submission. They destroyed crops and stores of food, set up blockades to interdict the flow of foodstuffs and starved more than a million Biafrans.[4] Throw in the effect of military defoliants and radiation from limited nuclear weapons, and we can project even more war-induced hunger and death.

If you are sickened by pictures of hollow-cheeked babies, bloated bellies, shriveled breasts and skeletal rib cages in the world press, brace yourself. The "famine century" is yet to climax. There are 950 million people who are hungry with 400 million of them on the verge of starvation.[5] Every year more than 20 million people die of starvation, malnutrition and hunger-related diseases including

40,000 children who die every day.[6] This means that forty-six people died of starvation since you started reading this section on famine.

2. A Whole Lot of Shakin' Going On

Jesus predicted that the increase of earthquakes would be one of the beginning signs of the end of the age. He had it nailed.

It's not that earthquakes are a new phenomenon. Antioch, Syria, not far from the place where Jesus gave His quake prediction, lost a quarter of a million people to a major earthquake in A.D. 526. Central China lost 830,000 in 1556. But a listing of recorded history's greatest quakes indicates that fifty-seven of the seventy-nine most lethal ones have occurred in the last eighty-three years. In fact, deaths from major quakes since 1900 total 1,283,000 — only 880,000 less than the *total death toll* from the previous fourteen centuries.[7] If you want an idea of the trend, the number of people killed in earthquakes in the seventies and eighties was 1148 percent the number killed in the fifties and sixties.[8]

Jesus specifically said that these end-time earthquakes would occur in various places, or in His words, "from place to place." In geographical distribution, all but one of the twenty-two major quakes recorded prior to 1900 occurred in Eurasia. But the fifty-seven biggies since the turn of the century have shaken up places as diverse as San Francisco and Tokyo, Guatemala and Algeria, China and Pakistan, Italy and Chile, Iran and El Salvador, the Soviet Union and Mexico.[9]

As I write this, workers are cleaning up from a massive 7.1 earthquake which took dozens of lives and caused several billion dollars' damage in the San Francisco area.

Almost simultaneously another quake hit China.

Excuse me while I slip out to take a couple of Excedrin tablets. I am sitting just a few miles from the southern end of the same fault line that shifted in the San Francisco Bay area, the San Andreas Fault. Scientists predict it could split at any moment, causing an 8.0 or greater quake, killing 80,000 people within fifty miles of my house. Whether or not they have read the prophecies, it would be tough to convince the people of San Francisco or the executives of my insurance company that earthquakes aren't increasing dramatically.

3. A Mess of Messiahs

I would be the first to affirm that the world is in desperate need of a messiah, a supernaturally endowed deliverer from the mess of the present age. But I never would have imagined that the demand for messiahs could dictate the supply. Messiahs seem to be trampling over each other to save the world.

From the Rev. Sun Moon to Lord Maitreya, from the son of a long dead pharaoh and Queen Nefertiti to Allen-Michael Noonan, more messiahs have appeared in the last thirty years than perhaps in any similar span of time in human history.

Dave Hunt has a fascinating catalog of self-appointed saviors in his book *Peace, Prosperity, and the Coming Holocaust.*[10] Hunt describes the following redeemers of the eighties:

Lord Maitreya

Lauded by his own "John the Baptist," Benjamin Creme, this "Lord" was the object of full-page ads in major world newspapers declaring, "THE CHRIST IS NOW

HERE." The ads, appearing the weekend of April 24-25, 1982, promised he would make himself known publicly within the next two months. Creme says this messiah is living in a Hindu-Pakistani section of southeast London and is waiting for the consciousness of the human race to be just right before revealing himself fully.

The UFO Saviors

Hunt declares:

> It is fascinating that so much of the literature involving UFOs has messianic overtones, including references to Christ. Alleged UFO contactees widely scattered around the world continue to receive messages about a coming messiah which are so similar that coincidence must be ruled out.[11]

As examples, Hunt describes the messianic transmissions from space being received by the Solar Light Retreat in Oregon and the messianic overtones of the teachings received from "space brothers" and published by the Mark-Age MetaCenter in Miami, Florida.

Allen-Michael Noonan

Allen-Michael Noonan heads the One World Family, claims to be in constant touch with extraterrestrials and declares himself to be God and messiah. He says he has been commissioned by "Venusians from the twelfth dimension" to help save the world, establish God's kingdom on this earth and spread the "Everlasting Gospel." He claims that galactic beings are planning to intervene in world affairs to bring about world unification through an artificial tribulation.

Jeanne Dixon's "Pharaoh Prince"

Jeanne Dixon claims to have had the most "significant and soul-stirring" vision of her life on February 5, 1962, the date which psychics and astrologers had long predicted would be the birthday of a new messiah. She saw a pharaoh and Queen Nefertiti offer a baby to the world and the peoples of the world surrounding him in worshipful adoration. Ms. Dixon says she believes a messiah was born that day, one that will "bring together all mankind in one all-embracing faith . . . the foundation of a new Christianity with every sect and creed united . . . the world as we know it will be reshaped and revamped into one without wars or suffering."[12]

If it were not for the sheer volume of independently derived and commonly focused content, one might be tempted to write off all of the above with the gurus and psychiatric-ward nuts of the world. But even if you write off their strange doctrines, you cannot deny either their claims to be saviors or their numerical strength. And these two features were the heart of Jesus' prediction, "*Many* will come in my name, *claiming to be the Christ,* and will deceive many."[13]

4. The Explosion of Explosions

Something strange has happened to warfare. Don't get me wrong—the object is still to annihilate as many of the enemy as possible as efficiently as possible. That hasn't changed, but the method of carrying out that objective has become radically different in the last thirty or forty years.

In the "good old days" of bloodshed, armies amassed their troops in rather well-defined geographical areas. Once there, they established rather clear lines facing each other and endeavored to blow the other guys to hell with firepower. This basic method of warfare prevailed from the very first recorded wars to the mid-twentieth century.

Not any more. In the middle of this century began the era of terrorist wars. In these wars you never quite know *where* the enemy is; he doesn't have nice, neat lines. You never know quite *who* he is; you can't even be sure he will be wearing a uniform. You never know quite *when* he will strike; he might attack only at night and pursue a regular job during the day or take a breather for a week. And you never can be sure you are *fighting a war;* it could be more like hit-and-run skirmishes spread over decades.

Vietnam was the first major conflict the U. S. got into in which the enemy fought under these new rules. It frustrated the army boots off our military. We knew if we could just get the enemy all together in one place in nice, neat lines like we were able to do in World War I, World War II, Korea and our earlier wars, we could blow them to kingdom come. But it didn't work that way. Vietnam was not a war. It was an endless series of skirmishes — a whole plethora of wars.

The global consequence of the communist specialization in terrorist warfare is that "event" wars have been replaced by "process" wars and "unit" wars have been pushed aside in favor of "series" wars. In short, the number of "wars" has increased exponentially.

How many wars are going on in the world today? Who knows? There are plenty of "event/unit" wars but a whole lot more "process/series" wars — wars in which you don't know whether you are warring or not except by the rumor mill. In Nam, they had a saying, "Vietnamese by day, Vietcong by night!"

Sound familiar? Jesus predicted not that there would be occasional "event" wars, but that in the final days there would be a *proliferation of wars and war rumors.*

He also predicted that this end-time proliferation would create more than just national, "kingdom against kingdom," wars. Jesus said there would be racial and ethnic wars as well. The word usually translated "nation" is the Greek word *ethnos* from which we get our word *ethnic.* Asia, Africa and the Middle East are filled with ethnic wars in addition to national ones. And you can collect a goodly number of political scientists who project that the ethnic factor will become so dominant that the U. S. and Russia might actually be lined up together against the Chinese, or the Chinese against the Japanese.

5. Laughing Uniformitarians

How would you like to give some leading religious and secular intellectuals a good laugh? I know a super way to do it.

With a straight face suggest you believe that at some specific, historic time the earth experienced a major, cataclysmic event which involved global, geologic upheavals and the inundation of the entire planet with water. Cite evidence from fossil remains of sea creatures at the top of Mount Everest. Describe unexplained, water-laid deposits miles deep (as in the Grand Canyon) with no observable process anywhere on earth for laying such massive deposits.

You can also suggest that the earth was once covered by a canopy of moisture creating a sort of global greenhouse and making it tropical. Describe how this could explain tropical, herbivorous animals getting quick-frozen into the ice of Siberia near the Arctic Circle.

If the intellectuals are not on the floor convulsing with laughter at this point, they either haven't understood you are serious or they are marked by unusual social courtesy. The majority of intellectuals view the world through an evolutionary and a uniformitarian matrix, and such notions appear ludicrous to them. Let me explain.

Thinking in evolutionary frameworks has spread far beyond the world of biological origins. I have sat in graduate school classes and heard professors try to prove that all religious thought has *evolved* in a near-Darwinian manner from simple to complex. This despite the fact that nothing ties thought processes together like the links between biological organisms.

Also foundational to the mindset of most intellectuals is a doctrine called *uniformitarianism.* This is the declaration that the physical dynamics governing the world order continue today *uniformly* as they have in the past. A favorite motto is, "The present is the key to the past."

This doctrine of uniformity seems pretty reasonable and harmless until you realize that, if enforced, it wipes out major keystones of biblical teaching and the Christian faith. If there is no room for cataclysms or dramatic, divine intervention in the natural order, then you can forget the notion of the flood of Noah with its geologic upheavals, the inauguration of the seasons at the end of that flood, the incarnation of God in human flesh, miracles, the resurrection and the second coming of Christ.

Does it strike you as significant that one identifying mark of the end of the age mentioned by two prophets and suggested by a third is uniformitarian thinking and widespread ridicule of any challenge to it?

Listen to an English paraphrase of one of the apostle Peter's prophecies:

First, I want to remind you that in the last days

there will come scoffers who will do every wrong thing they can think of, and laugh at the truth. This will be their line of argument: "So Jesus promised to come back, did He? Then where is He? He'll never come! Why, as far back as anyone can remember *everything has remained exactly as it was since the first day of creation*" [emphasis added].[14]

Make no mistake. According to the prophecies of the Holy Scriptures, a nearly global acceptance of uniformitarian thinking will mark the earth's last century. And if you are still smarting from the ridicule you received when you declared your belief in the biblical flood of Noah, take heart. The next paragraph of Peter's prophecy explains why you got those horse laughs:

They [the scoffers] deliberately forget this fact: that God *did destroy the world with a mighty flood,* long after He had made the heavens by the word of His command and had used the waters to form the earth and surround it [emphasis added].[15]

That these arrogant cynics are at work in the religious as well as the intellectual community is clear from Jude's prediction delivered to Christian believers:

In the last times there will be scoffers who will follow their own ungodly desires. These are the men who *divide you,* and follow mere natural instincts and do not have the Spirit [emphasis added].[16]

But, you may ask, *what makes you think that there are any more scoffing uniformitarians today than at other times in history?*

The intellectual world of this last century has so completely embraced the evolutionary hypothesis, and the Marxist world revolution has so thoroughly indoctrinated more than half of the world's people in uniformitarianism that it is now, since the early 1900s, the prevailing intellectual world view.

On a tour bus in the People's Republic of China, which, by the way, represents more than 20 percent of the world's people with its 1.1 billion population, the guide expressed his indoctrination with a smirk: "In China we don't believe in God or miracles; we believe in ourselves and hard work."

Once Again, With Feeling

We'll look at the sixth of the *beginning* pains in the four following chapters, but just to make sure we remember the first five let's review them:

1. A significant and widespread increase in famines.

2. A significant and widespread increase in earthquakes.

3. A dramatic increase in the number of phony messiahs.

4. A radical increase in national and ethnic wars and war rumors.

5. A predominance of intellectual and religious scoffers who ridicule the notion of the waning era of man or of any impending catastrophe.

Let me ask you: Do you think it is mere chance that these five dynamics have all converged as never before on one century of time after all the millennia of previous human history?

Yet the world is filled with "Mrs. Gullivers" who reject

the professional judgment of those who know what is going to happen. These "near term" Mrs. G's are "heading for Rio" in a state of denial because of their own long-standing plans for personal pleasure. They haven't "read the books," so they don't recognize the signs.

But it won't be long now. The *actual labor* will be upon them shortly—and it will hurt!

The apostle Paul, in one of his prophecies, declared:

> Now, brothers, about times and dates we do not need to write to you, for you know very well that the day of the Lord will come like a thief in the night. While people are saying, "Peace and safety," destruction will come on them suddenly, as *labor pains on a pregnant woman, and they will not escape* [emphasis added].[17]

While you're counting out the time between contractions on your wristwatch, it's important that we now examine the sixth *beginning* sign. It will help answer the question, "Are the earth's people really getting more and more evil, or is it my imagination?"

If you could master recognition of these *beginning* signs, think of the edge you would have on the rest of the world's citizenry. When the world begins to turn ugly on you, you'll understand what's happening and why. You'll see how everything falls into place in fulfillment of these amazingly accurate 2000-year-old predictions.

Stay with me. Our look at things to come may be frightening, but you owe it to yourself and your loved ones to be aware—and prepared. I promise you, there is light at the end of the tunnel.

5

A Good Man Is Harder to Find

"In fact, everyone who wants to live a godly life in Christ Jesus will be persecuted, while evil men and impostors will go from bad to worse, deceiving and being deceived."

Paul
2 Timothy 3:12,13

☐   ☐   ☐

Do you ever get this strange feeling that the collective morality of those in the world around you is deteriorating?

I know that people my age are expected to believe the younger generation is going to pot. But I happen to be a cockeyed optimist. Many have charged that one of my major faults is naively believing the best about others. I have an impressive array of uncollectible loans as evidence for their case.

But I must confess that I'm beginning to agree with those who wonder if morality in general is taking a catastrophic nosedive. It seems to me that the younger and older generations are *all* going to pot.

I am sure it doesn't help my perception to know that biblical prophets predicted a radical moral deterioration in the collective character of man at the end of the age. This sixth of the *beginning* of birth pains is described candidly by the apostle Paul in a prophetic message to young Timothy. Paul outlines what we can expect to see happen at the end of the eon:

> In fact, everyone who wants to live a godly life in Christ Jesus will be persecuted, while evil men and im-postors *will go from bad to worse,* deceiving and being deceived [emphasis added].[1]

A literal rendering of the Greek grammar in this prediction describes evil men "going forward to worse." Paul pictures a world marked by cruel inhumanity so great that it will make Hitler's Germany look like a pink lemonade party. This naturally would require a broader and deeper deterioration of the moral and ethical state of mankind, right? After all, we keep saying that we've learned our lesson from the Third Reich experience and that this "could never happen again."

I don't believe it.

A strange encounter I had some years ago started me thinking that perhaps people aren't getting more moral after all.

A Taxing Experience

I approached the entrance of the nondescript, beige-colored building with all the excitement of a man heading down Death Row to the Chair. All the building said on the front was "Internal Revenue Service." All the sign inside said was "Give your name, take a number and wait to be called." Less warmth than a dentist's office.

This was my first IRS audit. I suppose a psychologist would call my response to it "false guilt." It's the same feeling you have when you're followed for miles by a police car even though you know you're doing nothing wrong. I knew "to the best of my knowledge and belief" I had given correct and honest information on Form 1040. But, for some reason, that conviction wasn't chasing away my butterflies.

They called my name, and I lugged my filing system back into a small cubicle formed by those six-foot, free-standing partitions they euphemistically call "office landscaping." This "landscape" was bleak—a wonderland of blah beige.

The guy across the desk looked like a product of the sixties. His hair was unfashionably long. His attire was the "loose and wrinkled" look. On top of that he had an expression that made the Sphinx look like Dom DeLuise. If he had had a glass eye, I am sure it would have been the *warm* one.

Upon request, I paraded out a long series of documents. After each of my presentations, the agent would crunch away at his desk calculator and make another expressionless request for data. After about a half-hour of this process, during which I feigned comfortability and lightheartedness, he muttered something like, "Well, I guess everything looks all right."

"Does that mean the audit is finished?" I asked expectantly.

"Yes, with a few minor changes and a slight adjustment in the numbers here and there, we'll let your filing stand."

"Thank you, sir," I offered, trying to suppress my excitement. "May I make a suggestion which might help you in future audits?"

The agent looked up at me with a puzzled but I-guess-there's-no-harm-in-saying-yes look and nodded.

"Well, sir," I proceeded, "on the next audit like this I would suggest you check whether the moving expense has been reimbursed by the employer. You see, if I had wanted to take you, I could have done it on that matter and your audit would never have caught it."

He fell apart. The steady stoicism he had displayed earlier was gone.

"This is weird," he admitted. "You come in here cool and calm. You answer all of my questions, hiding nothing. You provide a set of documents which clearly supports your claims, and you totally disarm me so that I miss one of the biggest areas I should have checked. There's something *spiritual* about this!"

"There is, indeed," I responded quickly. "I am a follower of Christ and I guard the truthfulness of my actions out of obedience to Him and His law. That way I never have to fear someone like you checking my figures."

The Treachery Trend

The agent became thoughtful, almost philosophical, and leaned back in his chair.

"I don't usually do audits," he confessed, "but they pulled me off research to do this one. And I must say you are the exception to our trend."

"Your trend?"

"Yes. I've been doing research into the erosion of honesty in tax returns. This has been an area of increasing concern to the IRS. We've now documented that we are experiencing a 2 percent erosion of honest returns per year."

My mind went into "compute" mode. Even if you assumed that the 2 percent rate would not increase, in one decade an additional *one in five* Americans would be cheating on his tax. And this experience was more than a decade ago.

Since that encounter, my mind has raced back time and again to that prophetic word the apostle Paul gave to his protegé Timothy:

> But mark this: There will be terrible times in the last days. People will be lovers of themselves, lovers of money, boastful, proud, abusive, disobedient to their parents, ungrateful, unholy, without love, unforgiving, slanderous, without self-control, brutal, not lovers of the good, treacherous, rash, conceited, lovers of pleasure rather than lovers of God — having a form of godliness but denying its power. Have nothing to do with them.
>
> They are the kind who worm their way into homes and gain control over weak-willed women, who are loaded down with sins and are swayed by all kinds of evil desires, always learning but never able to acknowledge the truth.[2]

Larry, you may say, *that prophecy is no "sign" of end-time events. The world has always had people like this. Read history.*

I get your point. Paul's scary words are no "sign" if the characteristics described are more or less normative or distributed as they have been in previous generations. But

I don't think this prophecy is describing normalcy.

I once got a traffic ticket for not obeying a "no left turn" sign I didn't see. The sign was about 4 by 8 inches of fine print hanging from a wire twenty feet above an intersection. I appealed to the judge on a part of the law which says that to be prosecuted for not obeying a traffic sign, the sign has to be "clearly legible by an ordinarily observant person." The judge ruled in my favor.

I agree that if this last-days generation has about the same sprinkling of evil as other generations, then the sign would not be "clearly legible by an ordinarily observant person." Hence, no sign.

To be an indicating mark of an *historically unique generation,* these characteristics would have to differ from those of previous generations in two dimensions:

1. **Depth**: The evil would have to be markedly more extreme than ever before.

2. **Breadth**: The acceptance and practice of the evil would have to be significantly wider.

I believe the evidence exists that these two dimensions can be seen clearly in our generation.

Paul's prophecy, our sixth sign of the "beginning of birth pains," reveals twenty-one marks of end-time corruption. I have "repackaged" these into seventeen indicators which we will examine over this and the next three chapters. If it can be established that our generation has features which make it the best candidate for winner of the "Most-Likely-to-be-the-Last-Generation" contest, then our world is in deep trouble.

Join the esteemed panel of judges as I parade our generation before you. You will be asked to evaluate the candidate on the basis of seventeen categories. Do your best to be objective.

1. The Self-Lovers

If any generation ever took seriously the lofty ideal of the Golden Rule, it is definitely not this one. In their quest for personal self-satisfaction, many adults of the baby boom generation find themselves seemingly incapable of action that is not self-serving. This preoccupation with selfish concerns is typified in the goodbye letter written by a mother to her small boy in the movie *Kramer vs. Kramer*. Excusing her premeditated abandonment, she proclaims:

> I have gone away because I must find something interesting to do for myself in the world. Everybody has to and so do I. Being your mommy was one thing, but there are other things too.[3]

College students traditionally have been *avant-garde* in pursuing idealism, social justice and humanitarian causes at the expense of self-interest. As recently as the last twenty years, collegians have demonstrated for free speech, pullout from Vietnam, business divestitures in the Republic of South Africa, protection of the environment and racial equality.

All that is changing, according to a study done by the American Council of Education. Of the 290,000 college freshmen surveyed, only 57 percent were at all interested in helping people in difficulty compared with 68.5 percent in 1966. Only 27 percent expressed any concern about racial understanding, down from a meager 32 percent in 1985.[4]

So what are a majority of collegians interested in? Their own selfish pursuits. Marion Ryder, an honors senior at Bowdoin College, epitomizes the current ethos in explaining why he would not choose the medical profession: "Medical school would be a poor return on my investment."[5] In fact, in a 1987 study more than 75 percent of college freshmen perceived the goal of life to be *the accumulation of wealth*. Most indicated that the key reason they enrolled in college was to make more money. This contrasts with a figure of only 39 percent who thought that getting rich was an essential goal in a similar survey only twenty years earlier.[6]

Let's Hear It for #1!

In a rash of best-selling books, authors have captured and promoted the self-love dogma of our age. Robert J. Ringer, writing in *Looking Out for #1,* declares that a person's morals should be whatever gives him "enough money to be able comfortably to afford the material things [he wants] out of life."[7] Ringer also promoted his self-centered world view in the widely read book, *Winning Through Intimidation.*

Ringer exhorts his readers "to eliminate from your life all individuals who claim to possess [the right] to decide what is moral for you. You should concern yourself only with whether looking out for Number One is moral from your own rational, aware viewpoint."[8] Abandoning a friend with deep moral convictions is acceptable, even necessary, to advance your own goal pursuit, especially if the friend's values threaten you with feelings of discomfort or guilt.

Michael Korda proclaims this same self-exaltation in his book, *Success!* Korda declares:

> It's OK to be greedy. It's OK to look out for Number One. It's OK to be Machiavellian (if you can get away with it). It's OK to recognize that honesty is not always the best policy (provided you don't go around saying so).

It's *always* OK to be rich.[9]

Korda expands on his philosophy:

> The fastest way to succeed is to look as if you're playing by other people's rules while quietly playing by your own . . . Nobody minds ruthless, egocentric careerism and self-interest, provided they are suitably screened. If you can undermine your boss and replace him, fine, do so, but never express anything but respect and loyalty for him while you're doing it.[10]

C'mon, Larry, you may say, *these are just isolated and extreme examples of self-adoration. They do not indicate a generational pattern.*

You don't think so? Four practices that are freely accepted in our society tell me the opposite.

The Big Four

First, the divorce rate. I have done enough marriage counseling in my three decades of professional life to know that even in the "moral" or "religious" community most divorce is driven by self-interest. I believe that divorce statistics would drop instantly and dramatically if spouses could receive an injection of even a few cc's of selflessness.

Second, sexual promiscuity. Things like fornication and marital affairs could not exist if there were suddenly an epidemic of "doing unto others as you would have others do unto you." Despite all the palaver about "consenting adults," these illicit sexual relationships are inherently exploitive.

Third, the personal bankruptcy plague. Most of the people on my long list of "uncollectible loans" I mentioned earlier are there only because they have placed their personal self-interest above honor, fair play, contractual agreements, ethical considerations or the slightest concern for my well-being. Most get angry and act insulted when reminded about their obligations.

In our country, bankruptcy has become so commonplace and so widely free of stigma that there are currently 1.2 million bankruptcies in American courts, a post-depression high. The federal government recently added fifty-four new bankruptcy judges to handle the expanding volume. Losses to credit card companies from personal bankruptcies exceeded $10.8 billion in 1988 and are expected to reach $25 billion per year by 1995, if current trends continue.[11] And these aren't times of depression or even recession, but of economic prosperity. Many of these are "self-interest bankruptcies."

The news recently carried the story of a guy who drew cash against more than twenty credit cards to a sum totaling tens of thousands of dollars. He went to Las Vegas on the weekend, lost it all on one roll of the dice and returned home on Monday to file personal bankruptcy. Some will consider him clever or creative for this unusual action in his own self-interest. So acceptable has bankruptcy become that it has even become a pre-planned, wealth-gaining strategy for some real estate developers.

Fourth, the pro-abortion movement. All the bleating and whining about rapes, back alley abortions and coat-hanger deaths can't hide the fact that the vast majority of abortion decisions are not made in these contexts. They are made on the basis of *personal self-interest.* How much more need I say about self-love to a generation in which the basic, maternal instinct can be set aside casually and a mother's child can be sucked to pieces up a vacuum tube because the mother finds it embarrassing, undesirable, inconvenient, financially unfeasible or professionally restrictive to bear a child? Can there be any other basis for the "right to choose" but self-interest?

Have "Doing your own thing" and "I did it my way" ever had broader acceptance? Advertisers know that self-interest is in. Look at the rash of "You owe it to yourself," "Honor yourself" and even *Self* magazine themes.

Don't try to make it big with the premier edition of *Unselfishness* magazine — not in this generation.

2. Lovers of the Green

Coin, green stuff, moola, dough, cabbage, filthy lucre — what is it but a medium of exchange, the reward for our labor, a vehicle to fulfill our personal desires? And yet this generation has become a generation of Mammon worshippers.

In Columbus, Ohio, when $2 million in money bags and loose bills floated out of the back of a truck, pursuing motorists stopped and began stuffing their pockets. Only $100,000 of the $2 million was returned, $57,000 of it by an Ohio Bell repairman. When the repairman's father heard of his son's honest response, he was furious. He denounced the young man with the statement, "I thought I raised you better than that!"[12]

But this generation is more than petty thieves on the low-income end and corporate embezzlers on the other. This is a generation of larcenists at every level. Let's start at the top.

The betrayal of public trust is perhaps the worst sell-out of principle for money. But the erosion of public confidence in governmental institutions hasn't kept our nation's top government leaders from getting their hands in the till. As I write, the Speaker of the U. S. House of Representatives, the former director of the Housing and

Urban Development (HUD) department and the mayor of Los Angeles are under investigation for putting money ahead of morality. In the 1980s, more than 100 officials in government agencies were accused of misspending funds, perjury, using their positions for financial gain and other illegal acts. Some were found guilty and many resigned.

The chief of staff of the Department of Health and Human Services pleaded guilty to two felony conflict-of-interest charges. He funneled $55,000 of government money to himself and a private foundation. A Postal Service governor was declared guilty of expense account fraud and accepting kickbacks. An official of Health and Human Services and a Food and Drug Administration commissioner resigned after investigations into their travel expense reports.[13]

No Business Like Dough Business

In the past decade major defense contractors have been caught swindling the government out of hundreds of millions of dollars. Some of the corporations involved in financial misdealings have been trusted household names for generations. Hertz rental car agency pleaded guilty to overcharging customers and insurance companies for auto repairs following motorist accidents. The company paid a $6.9 million fine and agreed to pay full restitution to about 100,000 victims they had overcharged $13.7 million in seven years.[14] Even the Crayola crayon company was charged with secret price fixing with its major competitor.

But certainly you can trust your bank and your banker. After all, the banking industry must operate with the highest standards of trust in money matters, right? Wrong. A Comptroller of the Currency report found of the 189 U. S. bank failures from 1979 to 1987, fraud or insider abuse was a "significant factor" in 35 percent of the failures. Representatives of bank regulating agencies told a 1987 Congressional committee that among savings and loan failures, fraud was involved in almost half the cases, calling that level an "epidemic" of fraud.[15] Maybe your mattress and piggy bank weren't such unsafe places for your savings after all.

In 1988 an investigation by the House Commerce, Consumer and Monetary Affairs Subcommittee disclosed that the underreporting of income by American businesses to the IRS is so common that it probably costs the U. S. government up to $8 billion every year.[16]

But this shouldn't shock you. One-third of you reading this book have probably fudged on your income tax to gain a buck or two. Researchers into tax cheating have found that an additional third are either "receptive" or "ambivalent" to cheating on their taxes and have a "flexible definition of honesty."[17] Psychologist Russell Weigel of Amherst College observes that tax cheats have a "self-serving personality."[18] God has observed that they love money more than morality!

We collect the *stuff* money buys until our closets, cupboards and garages bulge. Comedian George Carlin has a hilarious monologue about people's *stuff*. If we get more money, we just buy more stuff or more expensive stuff, according to Carlin. Then we purchase storage sheds to house the overflow of stuff. When those burst at the seams, we rent storage compartments in which to stuff our stuff. Then it's a rental space for the skis, jet skis and RVs which we don't have room for (obviously) in either the garage or the driveway. We rent a spot at the marina for the boat and build a bigger house with more storage space for more stuff.

Tell me we don't love money and the stuff it buys.

And so we have it. Couples go into financial servitude

to pursue money and material things. Marrieds sacrifice time with the kids on the altar of material pursuits, chasing two (or more) jobs and the American dollar dream. Husbands become spiritual and emotional absentees from their wives and families to engage in corporate dollar chasing. Men and women fritter away their paychecks in pursuit of lottery prizes with the odds of winning the "big one" being one in millions. The worshippers of Donald Trump sell their souls to master the art of The Deal.

Money? We love the stuff enough to overwork, lie, steal, cheat and destroy for it.

But Larry, the U. S. is a paragon of virtue compared to the level of fraud, bribery and financial corruption found in many other nations.

Right you are. And that fact supports my point. The globe is wallowing in a cesspool of money-love. The international drug cartels have compromised the governments of scores of nations by sending a hit man to top officials with just one question, "Would you rather have silver or lead?" By the thousands, government leaders have chosen the silver. Silver they worship. The God who told us not to fear anyone who "has the power only to kill the body" they don't fear.

So I summarize this second indicator of end-time corruption by observing:

> Television moguls air the worst of violence and filth,
> If there is any chance at all of magnifying wealth.
> Kiddie porn kings twist lives and steal souls
> Of precious little children to promote financial goals.
> Junior highers steal the lives and even fry the brains
> Of friends, when selling crack brings them monetary gains.
> And one in three Americans, investigators find,

Cheat on their yearly income tax and rob their country
  blind.
Oh, Mammon, if you are not God and do not rule Lady
  Luck,
Then why do we bow down to you, just to make a buck?

For years I have complimented male friends with the
statement, "You're a good man." Then, after a slight pause,
I've added in jest, "There's just no demand for 'em." The
way the world is going, that line is losing its humor.

There's a crude, old joke about the drunk who calls
the Salvation Army and slurs, "Do you save bad girls?"
When the answer comes back in the affirmative, the drunk
mutters, "Good. Save me one for Saturday night." I'm sure
you've seen the bumper sticker, "Good Girls Go to Heaven;
Bad Girls Go Everywhere." The tragicomic end to all of this
is that at the end of the age — in this generation — there is
more demand for really bad girls than for truly good men.

The prophet could not have said it better when he said,
"At the end of the age, good men will be harder to find." I
believe he is describing *our* age with incredible precision,
and that the predicted trends will lead not only to a morally bankrupt society but also to a concerted persecution of
Christian believers across America and around the world.

But the prophet also tied the grand deliverance of all
humanity into this turning-point era — the rise of true goodness out of the darkness of deteriorating character.

How the internal condition of man
is fulfilling Paul's prophecy.

6

Is It Ever Hard to Find a Good Man!

"There will be terrible times in the last days. People will be lovers of themselves, lovers of money, **boastful, proud,** abusive, disobedient to their parents, ungrateful, unholy, **without love,** unforgiving, slanderous, without self-control, brutal, **not lovers of the good,** treacherous, rash, conceited, **lovers of pleasure rather than lovers of God**—having a form of godliness but denying its power. Have nothing to do with them."

Paul
2 Timothy 3:1-5

☐   ☐   ☐

It was one of the world's greatest civilizations. Its military power is legendary in the annals of conquest. Its engineers built roads, bridges, walled fortresses and aqueducts that are still in use today, two-and-a-half to three millennia later. Its concepts of government have influenced most of the nations of the Western world. Its language is still studied in Western high schools and colleges. Its art and architecture have left their imprint on design and structures over the globe. Its influence created an era of tranquility still legendary, the *Pax Romana.*

But the Roman Empire is extinct, as extinct as the whooping crane. Why?

As Edward Gibbons struggled to identify the causes for the collapse of this mighty colossus in his seventeen-volume classic, *The Rise and Fall of the Roman Empire,* he arrived at five factors:

1. The rapid increase in divorce.

2. The craze for pleasure.

3. The building of gigantic armaments when the enemy was within.

4. The increase in violence.

5. The decline of religion.

In short, Rome exhausted its decreasing supply of good people.

Civilizations often rise and fall on matters of character. Rome illustrated this principle: *External destruction follows internal decay.* Divorce destroyed the family. The pleasure craze upended right priorities. The arms race focused on the wrong enemy. Bloodthirstiness destroyed human civility. The decline of religion destroyed the foundation of the empire's values. Collapse.

Sadly, the prophets predict an end-time era of radical decline in virtue and moral character much more dramatic than Rome's. The decline starts out with more "benign" manifestations like self-love and money-love, seemingly victimless sins. But these reflect a striking and progressive internal decay which sets the stage for an awful outpouring of unspeakable persecution and violence.

To verify that this is true, and to prepare ourselves to stand strong in those trying times, let's continue our look at the seventeen indicators that our generation is fulfilling Paul's prediction that "everyone who wants to live a godly life in Christ Jesus will be persecuted while evil men and impostors will go from bad to worse, deceiving and being deceived."[1]

3. The Buzz Lovers

In his marks of the end of the age, the New Testament prophet merged numbers two and five on Gibbons's list: People will be lovers of pleasure rather than lovers of God. A California bumper sticker describes the motivation of our age, "In Search of the Eternal Buzz."

It's confession time.

I collect and operate old toy trains. I have more trains in my basement and garage than I care to acknowledge. I have been known to travel three-fourths of the way across this continent to attend the world's largest toy train meet. I have also been known to pay good sums of money for a rare, pre-1920 relic from the Lionel Train Company. I get a "buzz" out of my hobby.

But my hobby is just a hobby. It does not consume my life, my time, my passions or my money. Relationships are still more important to me than trains. My vocational pursuits are still more important to me than my trains. I am not in debt for a single toy train. God is the owner of the collection, and He knows I will sell it in a minute if He so directs. My love for trains isn't even in the same league as my love for Him!

But I find that I am in the minority in the train-collecting world. I am viewed as somewhat of an oddity for my "take it or leave it" attitude toward my hobby. The club leadership couldn't understand the problem when I objected to their moving meetings from Friday evening to Sunday mornings. They assumed I was just miffed that, as a minister, I couldn't attend. I guess it never occurred to them that I might love God more than trains.

The prophet described the last days as "marked by people who were in love with pleasure *at the expense of* their love for God." The grammatical construction indicates that these people have performed a horse trade: "God love" for "pleasure love."

I don't have to draw you a picture on this one. Across the world the pursuit of pleasure at the expense of faith is the rule rather than the exception. A leading humanist postulated that one of only three reasons anybody attends church is that they don't play golf.

T. G. I. F.

If you have any doubt about the prophet's picture being a radically accurate description of contemporary American society, I'll take you with me out to the freeway from Los Angeles to Las Vegas some Friday evening. There we can watch the bumper-to-bumper traffic for the four-hour drive to Pleasure City. Or we can sit by another freeway heading toward Palm Springs and the desert. There we will watch the endless parade of RVs, trailers with boats, trailers with ATCs, trailers with jet skis, trailers with dirt bikes, trailers with dune buggies, trailers with drag racers, trailers with race cars, mobile homes, mobile homes pulling 4x4s, off-road pickups and campers.

As if these buzz seekers are not going to get sufficient pleasure out of their vehicles, they are loaded down with alphabet stuff. TVs, VCRs, CBs and CDs to go with their RVs, ATCs and BMXs. To further enhance their pleasure, many carry boom boxes, bikinied beauties, beer barrels and brain boosters.

If you think this weekend ritual is going to include a visit to a place of worship or even a personal devotional time as a top priority, think again. These people — many of them professing Christians — traded God in for pleasure a long time ago, and they aren't about to trade back.

In the most church-going nation in the world, six out of ten still prefer pleasure to piety.[2]

4. Lacking in Good-Love

Listen in on a missionary to Indonesia describing his attempt to tell cannibalistic nationals the story of Christ:

> I expanded further on the life and ministry of Jesus, trying to establish His reality and relevance to their lives, but without apparent success. The Sawi were not accustomed to projecting their minds into cultures and settings so forbiddingly dissimilar from their own.
>
> Only once did my presentation win a ringing response from them. I was describing Judas Iscariot's betrayal of the Son of God. About halfway through the description I noticed they were all listening intently. They noted the detail: for three years Judas had kept close company with Jesus, sharing the same food, traveling the same road.
>
> That any associate of Jesus would have conceived the idea of betraying such an impressive figure was high-

ly unlikely. And if anyone *had* conceived the idea, one of Jesus' inner circle of trusted disciples would have been the least likely to choose such a course . . . .

At the climax of the story, Maum whistled a birdcall of admiration. Kani and several others touched their fingertips to their chests in awe. Still others chuckled.

At first I was confused. Then the realization broke through. *They were acclaiming Judas as the hero of the story!*[3]

In order for any society to keep from "turning ugly," there has to be a basic love and appreciation for that which is good. In the above narrative from Don Richardson's *Peace Child,* Don reflects the incredible contempt that the New Guinea Sawi people had for goodness. Judas, not Jesus, was the object of their admiration and awe for his cunning, his clever deception, his creative barbarism. Jesus was good, but the Sawis valued treachery, not goodness. So Judas was their Superman.

The prophetic word to young Timothy was that in the last days people would have no affection for what is good. Some translators word this "good-haters." By implication, the apostle Paul is declaring that the more good you are in that generation, the less affection you will receive from those around you.

99 and 44/100 Percent Impure

Welcome to the twenty-first century! We are reaching this level fast. A number of years ago I publicly expressed disapproval of the fact that astronauts on the Apollo Ten mission to the moon had used such filthy language and impure expletives that NASA secretaries refused to transcribe them. In a telegram to then-President Nixon, I requested a public apology for this behavior.

Did I ever get flayed! Hundreds of hate letters, scores

of vicious phone calls, acidic talk show hosts and even some veiled threats on my life let me know that people in this society don't want anyone around with standards that are too good. They'll tolerate goodness only as long as it doesn't conflict with their arbitrary ratio of goodness to evil. They may call it "naughtiness," "sophistication" or "adult entertainment," but they don't want it to get a "G" rating. That would be the kiss of death.

Donald Wildmon gets pilloried by the press in vicious columns and media diatribes for his righteous stand against pornography. Anita Bryant had so many bomb threats and such violent abuse heaped on her for her stand against legislating homosexuality that it cost her her career and was a factor in costing her her marriage. Terry Rakolta, the Michigan homemaker who protested the primetime filth of Fox Television's *Married With Children,* is a curse word in the world of electronic media.

Listen to an increasingly typical opinion from a columnist who doesn't share the Christian's love for goodness. His ire was stirred by the protest against the movie *The Last Temptation of Christ* which showed Jesus fantasizing a sex act with Mary Magdalene. He wrote the following in the Orange County, California, *Register,* referring to Christian protesters as "Those Who Know Better":

> Let's suppose for a minute that the movie is more or less blasphemous, whatever that means.
>
> Let's suppose the movie does portray Christ as a sex-starved lout, as some of Those Who Know Better charge. Let's suppose the movie does mock Jesus. Let's suppose the movie does raise questions about whether Jesus is the son of God. Let's suppose the movie does contain, gasp, sex and nudity. Let's suppose all of this is true.
>
> So what?
>
> I still ought to be able to go see it without a bunch

of holier-than-thou twits telling me it's not good for me.

After all, one man's blasphemy is another man's piety, and the Constitution protects it all.

The problem with Those Who Know Better is that they actually think they do . . .[4]

Did you feel the cutting knifeblade of hatred for goodness? It's getting sharper everywhere. Try speaking against the porn stars defending their lifestyle on *Donahue*. Blow your horn at the pickup ahead of you when the driver dumps litter over the highway. Refuse to fudge on your expense account thereby revealing the corruption of other employees. Or take the pulpit from your minister some Sunday and preach a strong biblical message on the evils of divorce and remarriage.

The responses won't be pretty. And they're getting uglier by the minute.

5. Pride Puffed

Passing a local dry cleaning establishment years ago, I noticed the message on the changeable sign out front: "If the Meek Inherit the Earth, Who Will Drive All the Trucks?" While the sign made a point, truckers don't have a corner on the arrogance traffic of our time. We all share in that.

I have seen persons of high estate flaunting themselves in the midst of their wealth, beauty and power: Donald and Ivana Trump showing the TV cameras their $200 million, 300-foot yacht with its movie theater, swimming pool, two 30-foot speed boats, onyx masterbath, eleven double-sized staterooms, 210 telephones and three elevators. I presume they flaunt their personal Boeing 727 as well.

I have also seen jungle Indians who owned a hut and

a few cooking pots swagger through the village half-naked, parading their physical strength, freshly created "beauty marks" or the game from a successful hunt.

Pride knows no cultural or social boundaries.

We can also be assured that no end-time generation is responsible for inventing pride. The prophetic picture in retrospect reveals that pride was found in one high-ranking and ambitious angel named Lucifer. Hanging around ever since, pride is a universal "given."

The "last days character list" includes *three* forms of human arrogance. The prophet pictures "three-dimensional" arrogance in the three Greek words he chose:

1. Boasting and bragging

2. Conspicuous self-elevation

3. Inflation, as with conceit

These words remind me of an inflatable toy doll with a mind of its own. First, the doll repeatedly pushes a foot pump to fill itself with air—undoubtedly *hot* air. Now fully inflated, the doll begins strutting through the community, boasting loudly about its features and professing to possess substance. Finally, the doll fights for a social position elevated high above all others. Having reached that lofty position, it is oblivious to the fact that it still is nothing but a bag of wind.

The apostle Paul portrays the last era as populated with fully inflated toy dolls, puncturing each other to gain prominence, inflating themselves to the bursting point and cranking up the volume on their loudspeaker systems to deafen all rivals with self-praise.

Sounds a lot like some cocktail parties I've attended—

and maybe even a ministerial meeting or two.

Humility? "Blessed are the meek"? "Humble yourself in the sight of the Lord"?

Forget it. This generation despises humility.

6. Frigidity

I nearly wept as I poured through the chapters of the book. For a clean living, virginal, Christian kid who had never visited or known a lady of the evening, this psychological case study of prostitutes was a killer. Had it not been an assignment for my college criminology class, I doubt I could have finished it.

One after another, these tortured human beings shared their thoughts and feelings with the psychologists and psychiatrists interviewing them. After reading half-a-dozen or so of these case studies, I realized these women were the same in one respect: They had *lost their ability to love.*

Many of these women, abused and rejected in childhood, had early sought affection and acceptance so desperately that they gave sex to get love. When they discovered man after man who gave love only to get sex, they became hurt and disillusioned, then resentful and bitter and, finally, hard and incapable of loving.

Ever since these women made the marriage act a business practice erroneously called "making love," something in their human spirits had died. It was the ability to give and receive genuine love.

The apostle Paul forecasts one of the most frightening features of the end time: the *inability to love.* He uses a word, *non-cherishing,* which can be paraphrased, "without the ability to cherish anyone." One translation describes this gaping hole in the human psyche as "without natural affection."

A second prophetic utterance projects the same image. Jesus, in His most expansive prophetic vision of the end of the age, declares, "Because of the increase of lawlessness the love of most will grow cold."[5] An expanded paraphrase of this statement might be, "After engaging in such consistent and flagrant violation of God's laws, the vast majority of people will lose the capacity to feel and express warm commitment to anyone; that ability will 'go cold' on them."

The Global Icebox

It is a natural, bodily defense mechanism for a callous to form on an area of skin where potentially injurious rubbing occurs. It is also a defense mechanism of the human spirit to "freeze" the capacity to love when the vulnerability of loving puts the spirit in danger of injury.

At this point the character profile of the terminal age becomes anything but benign. It is love that makes the world a tolerable place to live. It is a societal core of loving goodwill, warm affection and self-sacrificing commitment that turns the ordinarily hostile environs of planet Earth into a place of relative joy.

Without this consensus of affection, warmth and trust, the world will be spiritually quick-frozen into an intolerable place. Lovelessness will flow like liquid hydrogen over humanity, making every person "breaking-point brittle" to the least provocation.

There is powerful evidence we are headed this way.

New York City looks back a quarter-century to a case that seasoned New Yorkers say marked the beginning of the end of decency. The incident shocked Americans into recognizing we had developed a calloused heart. It was the

Kitty Genovese case.

For more than half-an-hour, thirty-eight respectable, law-abiding citizens in Queens watched a killer stalk and stab Kitty in three separate attacks. After the first attack, Kitty screamed, "Oh my God, he stabbed me." After the final attack came the vain shriek, "I'm dying. I'm dying." Citizens in the apartment building across the street opened windows to look. Others closed windows to deaden the noise of scuffling and screaming. All in all, not one of the thirty-eight witnesses did one thing to protect, defend or save Kitty.[6] Any way you view it, the love of thirty-eight human beings for one of their own had grown cold.

This hideous lovelessness was replayed more recently in Central Park where a number of teen boys repeatedly raped and beat a young woman for fun in an exercise they called "doing the wild thing."

There you go again, Larry, citing an anecdote or two from which you generalize to the whole society. This doesn't mean the whole world is increasingly loveless.

Author Isaac Bashevis Singer, winner of a Nobel Prize for literature, agrees with me. He declares society to be increasingly callous, its compassion waning and its people largely unable or unwilling to develop relationships of trust:

> I'm also in despair because people take what is happening for granted. They read about thousands of people being destroyed, and then they turn to the stock tables as if nothing had really happened. People take the attitude: "It happens to other people; it's not going to happen to me." In that way, I would say that civilization has hardened men's hearts more than it has softened them.[7]

In Jesus' perspective on this end-time phenomenon, He attributed spiritual and emotional frigidity to the in-

creased incidence of people breaking the laws of God. I
think this can be documented in our time and place.

Friend, I hope you are a sensitive, trusting, sweet-
spirited follower of God's law and are personally related to
the Son of God. This grim portrayal of evil, end-time trends
does nothing but make you shine more and more brightly
by contrast. God can see it, too, and has plans to protect
and reward you for your faithfulness.

Don't lose heart.

The Divorce Harvest

Divorce is condemned in the Scriptures because it violates one of man's most significant contractual relationships — the one he has with his spouse. The Old Testament
prophet Malachi declares boldly:

> You flood the Lord's altar with tears. You weep and
> wail because He no longer pays attention to your offer-
> ings or accepts them with pleasure from your hands. You
> ask, "Why?" It is because the Lord is acting as the wit-
> ness between you and the wife of your youth, because you
> have broken faith with her, though she is your partner,
> the wife of your marriage covenant.
>
> Has not the Lord made them one? In flesh and spirit
> they are His. And why one? Because He was seeking godly
> offspring. So guard yourself in your spirit, and do not
> break faith with the wife of your youth.
>
> "I hate divorce," says the Lord God.[8]

So do I.

I believe that divorce is the single most significant factor in the growing lovelessness and emotional frigidity of
our age. Because marriage — and the spiritual and sexual
oneness which it creates — affects the human psyche and
spirit so deeply, the destruction of that relationship leaves

nearly irreparable damage to those involved. As a twice-married friend of mine observed, "When you say 'until death do us part,' that's the way that decision is going to affect you *whether you like it or not!*" For spouses, the damaging effect of a divorce is inevitable injury to the capacity to love and trust.

Because the relationship between parent and child is the single most powerful dynamic in shaping a child's personality and forming patterns of emotional expression and repression, the breach of that relationship through divorce renders the child incapacitated in loving or trusting as well.

"Intimacy requires consummate trust. And today, trust is in short supply," writes Carl Avery in a *Psychology Today* article titled, "How Do You Build Intimacy in an Age of Divorce?" "With one of two marriages ending in divorce . . . trusting someone to be committed over the long haul is increasingly difficult."[9]

Drs. Connel Cowan and Melvyn Kinder of the Center for Relationship Studies observe that the high divorce rate accounts for much of the difficulty people have in trusting others. They note that people "do not give freely, but conditionally, from fear that a relationship will not last."[10] That fear translates into an incapacity to love and trust.

One long-term study measured the effects of divorce on children. At three stages—eighteen months, five years and ten years after the family break-up—the children manifested a "sleeper effect." Even the adult children, between ages nineteen and twenty-three, feared commitment and had trouble developing deep relationships. Two-thirds of the women indicated clearly that residual fears and anxieties from their parents' divorces hindered their own relationships.[11]

The Love Freeze

Jesus of Nazareth predicted, "the love of most will grow cold." I believe this emotional frigidity is in large part the harvest of marital disobedience sown earlier. With quick and easy divorce now totaling over a million a year in the U. S. and becoming an international phenomenon, it will create what I believe will be a global "love freeze."

Add to the divorce victims the increasing percentage of people unable to love or trust because of childhood physical abuse, sexual abuse and incest, and the number of the love-frozen becomes even more substantial.

Then factor in the millions of adult children of alcoholics. These traumatized people, according to Janet G. Woititz, president of the Institute for Counseling and Training, "simply do not know how to have a healthy, intimate relationship" because they "fear intimacy and are deeply frightened of being abandoned."[12]

And compound this number with those who are completely compassionless because they have been desensitized by feeding on the most explicit and ghoulish media violence to the tune of 18,000 killings witnessed per childhood.

There is hardly a vestige of TLC left in anyone.

Regardless of the circumstances creating it, there is nothing like a devastating breach of trust by someone you love (and whom you think loves you) to cool your ability to love again. An old American proverb proclaims, "A scalded cat runs from cold water."

Dr. Ken Magid and Carole A. McKelvey portray a whole generation of the love-frozen in their book, *High Risk — Children Without a Conscience.* Their research discovered a vast number of children displaying "affectionless psychopathy" marked by symptoms such as preoccupation with fire, blood or gore, cruelty to others or animals, abnormalities in eye contact, self-destructive behavior, inability and unwillingness to trust anyone, the absence of a developed conscience and lack of ability to give and receive affection. These children get satisfaction from hurting others, express no remorse if caught and exploit a person's vulnerability with no regrets.[13]

The causes of this frightening social and psychological pathology are precisely the ones I cite above. This "affectionless psychopathy" is caused by what Magid and McKelvey call "Pathogenic Parenting." This is defined as "discontinuity of parenting that arouses unconscious resentment and anger which persist into adult life and ultimately find expression in the mistreatment of those who are weaker."[14]

Trust me, it won't be pleasant to live in a world in which all these children traumatized by divorce, abuse, incest, alcoholism and abandonment are living and growing up. It will be a spiritual Arctic, a loveless, emotionally frigid world.

Should the magic of love "freeze up" across the world, this whirling sphere will become a global torture chamber filled with emotionally cold executioners. This kind of world is the setting the prophet predicts for an avalanche of violent, unrestrained, hate-motivated persecution.

In this horrific scenario a good man becomes the hated and the damned. He'll need divine care and sustenance to survive and to conquer. Will it be there for him when he needs it?

7

The Bad Guy Glut

"There will be terrible times in the last days. People will be lovers of themselves, lovers of money, boastful, proud, abusive, **disobedient to their parents,** ungrateful, unholy, without love, unforgiving, **slanderous,** without self-control, **brutal,** not lovers of the good, **treacherous, rash,** conceited, lovers of pleasure rather than lovers of God — having a form of godliness but denying its power. Have nothing to do with them . . . Evil men and impostors will go from bad to worse, **deceiving and being deceived.**"

Paul
2 Timothy 3:1-5,13

☐   ☐   ☐

The airplane had taxied to the terminal, and the mad rush into the aisles *much* before the seat belt light had been extinguished indicated that this was a third world flight. I had never been to Lagos, Nigeria, before, so I had little idea what to expect.

An American businessman in front of me in the aisle began to mutter to himself like a psychotic. I couldn't help hearing the most awful string of four-letter words I'd heard in a long time, delivered with increasing bitterness and volume. Finally, I couldn't restrain myself any longer.

"Excuse me, sir," I interrupted, "Is something wrong?"

"!@#*!," he responded, "I told my boss I would never come to this #*!@ place again, but here I am."

"Why did you say 'yes'?" I asked rather innocently.

"Oh, he offered me more !#%@! money, and I bit for it!"

The line moved. The man continued swearing and muttering as we inched toward the cockpit.

It can't be that bad, I thought to myself as I neared the exit door where the flight attendant was bidding adieu to the passengers. She had a deeply pained expression, not the pleasant smile that had greeted me upon exit from hundreds of other flights. As our eyes met, she spoke with the kind of empathy one friend might express for another when facing death or destruction.

"Do you really want to get off here?" she asked. There was not the least hint of humor in her voice.

"Is it *really* that bad?" I returned.

"It is *really* that bad."

"Well, I guess I'm here now," I half-laughed as I started down the portable steps, reassuring myself once again that it couldn't *really* be that bad.

It was *really* that bad.

24-Hour Hell

Jean Paul Sarte, the French existentialist, wrote a depressing play in which he portrays hell as a room into which an endless string of evil, ill-motivated people are delivered. Titled *No Exit,* the play captures, in frightening ways, the horror of being held in a place where you could never escape from evil people. Discounting a lake of fire, weeping, wailing and gnashing of teeth, such a collection of people quickly makes hell *hell.*

The twenty-four hours I spent after disembarking from that airplane were the closest I have ever come to being in hell. For those of us who have come to expect a common denominator of goodness, goodwill, ethical operation, respect and trust in our relatively secure rural or suburban communities, we have little idea what it is like to live in Harlem, in hell or in Lagos.

That one day was filled with a variety of terrors, the least of which included being glared at by humanity at every level of society from immigration official to taxi driver and being treated like scum by the rest.

Trust based on ethics was non-existent. The pre-reserved and pre-paid reservation at the airport hotel turned mythical because someone had bribed someone else to take it away from us. The travel agent had warned us that if the reservation did not exist (his prediction) no refund would be forthcoming (the outcome). The hotel lobby was jammed to the walls with bitter, disgruntled, aggressive people standing guard over their possessions to protect them from the larcenous intentions of covetous people everywhere. Two American missionaries checking out of the hotel told me of fighting off an intruder in their room in the middle of the night—an intruder who escaped with many of their most valuable possessions including their wedding rings.

After offering a higher price for a taxi than the others waiting at the curb, we were taken to another "hotel" where we were charged five times the going rate for a filthy, infested room with a "private bath." When we discovered the "private bath" had no running water in either sink, shower or toilet, we reported the matter to the man behind the desk. He let out a cackle reminiscent of a horror movie villain, heaping derision on us for having the stupidity to believe that the "private bath" was really going to be a *functioning* private bath. He sneeringly handed us a bucket.

My traveling companion and I selected a second floor room mainly for security reasons and piled furniture against the door. Good thing. More than once in the night we heard the door knob and door being worked for possible entry.

A fitful night trying to sleep in the torridly humid weather. A hair-raising ride to the airport amidst cursing, glaring, teeming humanity. Visions of the dirt, disarray, dinge, deterioration, destruction, demolition and defecation. A metropolis rendered largely inoperative by the stripping of every valuable, usable item that could be carried off. A region where you don't stop at night on the highway for a fallen tree or even a prostrate body on the road lest it be a trap set by roadside bandits. A place where auto steering wheels are locked with iron bars, accessories are commonly stripped off and hubcaps are only temporary.

The lift-off of our plane the next day was deliriously joyful. I am sure that commercial craft must have sky-written *THANK GOD* on its way out of Lagos air traffic control. Be assured that was the prayer I breathed as I settled back in my seat.

I recount this because most of us living outside the slums have no idea what life is like when "evil men go from bad to worse." We are going to find out.

The apostle Paul went far beyond the *self-loving, money-mad, pleasure-crazed, good-hating, arrogance-filled, love-frozen* adjectives to describe this last of all pre-judgment generations. These conditions focused largely on the *internal* state of mankind. When describing *how people would relate to each other,* the prophet chose even more vicious descriptions. Try *slanderous, rash, brutal* and *treacherous* on for size.

7. Superslander

Jerry Falwell loves and respects his godly mother. He felt certain that the courts would defend her from a vicious and totally false character attack by Larry Flynt's pornographic *Hustler* magazine. *Hustler* portrayed Falwell's mother in a manner not suitable for recounting in this book. Suffice it to say that the magazine used the most vicious of moral slurs against her in a cartoon feature. In keeping with our cultural redefinition of acceptable "free speech," this libelous attack was protected even by the U.S. Supreme Court.

Supermarket tabloids publish false accusations about prominent figures so often that Hollywood stars have begun to take them in stride. Few have the time, money or spirit to hold the tabloids accountable for the increasingly vicious untruths they publish weekly. A rare exception was Carol Burnett, who pressed her case against *The National Enquirer* and won a multimillion dollar judgment.

These end-time slanderers are not limited to the tabloids; they are characteristic of the age. The Greek word the prophet used is *diabolos.* If that word seems vaguely similar to the Spanish word for devil, there is good reason. The word is translated "devil" thirty-five of the thirty-eight times it is used in the New Testament. The other three times it is "false accuser" or "slanderer."

Get the picture? The last generation will be marked by people who operate just as Satan did when he stirred false accusations resulting in the crucifixion of Christ. It won't matter whether the accusations are true. It won't matter whether they are character assassination. It won't even matter if they result in the unjust persecution of the accused. All that will matter is that the slander serves the purposes of the slanderer.

I know what I am talking about. In a lawsuit against me a man fabricated telephone logs of nonexistent phone conversations with me and *presented them to the court as evidence*, quoting me as taking full financial responsibility for hundreds of thousands of dollars worth of obligations which were not even mine.

If you don't think that slander has become a common practice in this generation, spend a little more time in a divorce court.

8. Make My Day!

"Go ahead. Make my day!" has become a byword of the hostile society. In case you are not familiar with the origin of this statement, it was first spoken by actor Clint Eastwood playing Dirty Harry in the movie *Sudden Impact*. Fingering a gun and itching for a chance to use it to blow the other guy away, Dirty Harry challenges, "Go ahead. Make my day." Interpretation: "I dare you to give me an excuse to blow you to pieces. To have the opportunity to do so would make my day."

While this attitude may make dramatic movie action, it would not "play well" in real life. But playing it is. The prophet predicted that the last generation would be "rash," using a compound word literally meaning "falling forward" or "headlong." We would describe it as "heady" or "headstrong" or "brash."

Swaggering machismo. Defiant daring. Intimidating verve. "Don't-mess-with-me-buddy" panache. The Don Rickels/Joan Rivers syndrome. Gum-chewing Roseanne Barr of TV's *Roseanne* series whining, "My husband said he needed a little space, so I locked him out of the house." The husband and wife on *Married with Children* verbally ripping each other apart before their children and neighbors. Both shows tops in the ratings. *Rash.*

Rashness not the mark of our age? Have you talked to veteran public school teachers or administrators lately? Ask them about the insolent "I-dare-you-to-mess-with-me" attitude in schools now compared with the first years they taught. Interview people who have related to the public by profession for a few decades, and see if they do not confirm the existence of current, record-breaking levels on the "brashness scale."

And don't feel like you are the only one on the receiving end of this increase in smart-mouthed arrogance. God is getting His share, too. In another adjective used by the prophet, he describes the final era as "abusive," the word *blasphemoi* in Greek. Yes, you caught it. Those who are brash with other human beings are "blasphemers," railing against God. This explains why "Jesus Christ" is the only personal name I know used commonly as an expletive in this society. This helps us understand why "My God" and "God Damn" are also on the top ten list of swear phrases.

The driver who pushes you off the road. The senior citizen who elbows into line in front of you at the supermarket. The biker who gives you an obscene street gesture at the least provocation. The teenager who gives you an earful of four-letter words because he doesn't like your looks.

This is the *Rash* Generation — filled with people who want you to "make their day."

9. Brutality By Any Other Name . . .

Item: The citizens of our community were revulsed when a couple tortured their two-year-old child, burning him within an inch of his life by repeatedly pressing a lighted cigarette into his flesh.

Item: A young boy named Robbie told his social worker the following about his mother:

> The scariest is when she gets into certain moods. Oh, boy. First, there's kind of a buildup while she gets madder and madder. Then she grabs me, knocks me around for awhile and eventually knocks me down on the floor. Then while I'm lying on the floor, she has these high-heeled shoes, real pointed shoes with spiked heels, and she kicks me while I'm lying there. Sometimes I get kicked in the face, but usually it's everywhere else — it looks too bad afterward when she kicks me in the face.[1]

Item: In Corpus Christi, Texas, a twelve-year-old boy shot a stockbroker on a crowded, downtown street. The wounded stockbroker could not understand the kid's nonchalance. After the shooting, the boy "blew the smoke out of the gun barrel, Clint Eastwood style, then got on his bike and drove away."[2]

Item: In an interview in South Central Los Angeles, a gang leader casually admitted he had killed a number of people. When asked if he felt any guilt or remorse, he assured the interviewer that he didn't, that "you don't feel nothin'."

Item: Karen Toshima, a twenty-seven-year-old graphic artist, was with her boyfriend for an evening out in fashionable Westwood, California. They planned to "have a good time, look in the stores, grab a Coke and just look around," said her brother Kevin. At 10:45 P.M. she was felled by a bullet to the head, an innocent victim of gang-related violence.[3]

Item: In Carl Junction, Missouri, a small, mostly God-fearing community, the high school student body president and a few close friends repeatedly stabbed and bashed the skull of one of their friends until he was dead. As the bludgeoning proceeded, the victim screamed repeatedly, "Why me, you guys? Why me?" "Because it's fun, Steve," they replied. After the murder the killers cleaned the blood off themselves, changed clothes and routinely joined their families for dinner.[4]

Larry, there you go again with the "isolated-instance" approach to making your point. You could get thousands of "items" that still wouldn't prove a trend.

Thanks for reminding me. I realize that I could "anec-dote you" to death with cases of violence and brutality in a country as large as ours, so let me have you take a step back so we can look at the overall picture. After all, the New Testament prophet said that "brutality" would be a characterizing mark of the end of the age, using a word also translated "savage" and "fierce."

The Brutality Boom

Rates of violent crime in the nation's largest cities rose 43 percent from 1977 through 1987. Lest you think that this savagery can be explained by population growth, that decadal rate represented a 22 percent increase in violent crimes per 100,000 of population. This Violent Crime Index includes murder, negligent manslaughter, rape, robbery and aggravated assault.[5] The murder rate had *doubled* in 1980 from the level in 1960. Louis West of the UCLA School of Medicine declared, "Here's a country that's having an epidemic [of violence]."[6]

By any chance do you have a young person in your home? So violent has the society become that the U.S. Bureau of Justice Statistics predicts that 83 percent of children age twelve or under will become victims of actual or attempted violence sometime in their lives if crime trends continue.[7] In fact, in the mid-1980s violent death, including suicide, was the *leading cause* of death for young people ages fifteen through twenty-four.

If you think your son or daughter will be safe at school, think again. Every day 135,000 students come on school campuses carrying guns. Many schools have completely removed lockers to eliminate hiding places for drugs and weapons. To eliminate guns, fifteen New York City schools now require kids to enter through metal detectors. Each year, three million crimes occur on school grounds. More than 184,000 students, faculty and administrators were injured last year.[8]

As I ate breakfast and glanced over today's newspaper *an hour before I wrote these paragraphs,* I read on the front page, "Boy Shoots Fellow Student During Siege in Anaheim."[9] A teenager took over a high school drama class and shot a kid who dared him to do so.

Brutal.

Wait a minute, Poland. Reading this is depressing. For three chapters now I've been looking for the "happy ending." Is there one?

There is one, a great one. It's coming. But I need for you to hold on a little while longer so you'll see clearly how all the pieces are fitting into place for the end of our world as predicted in the Holy Scriptures. It's a tough ride, I know. But believe me when I tell you you'll be glad you stayed aboard!

Unfortunately, our homes aren't protected from the wave of savagery that is promised in the persecution to come. The number of *reported* cases of child neglect and abuse in 1985 was 1.3 million, representing 1.93 million children.[10] Since police estimate that for every case reported, two or three actual abuses occur, as many as 5.8 million children were probably abused in 1985 with the most common abuses being deprivation of necessities, physical injury and sexual maltreatment.[11]

Every eighteen seconds a woman is battered in her home, totaling four million women a year. This brutality crosses all socio-economic barriers, "every race, ethnic group and religion . . . doctors, lawyers, policemen and judges are abusers. So are unemployed men on the streets," asserts Kathleen Gerety, a program director at Battered Women's Service in Danbury, Connecticut.[12]

10. Home, Not-So-Sweet Home

If biblical prophecies mean anything, there may be real substance underlying two bumper stickers frequently seen around Southern California: "Insanity Is Hereditary; You Get It From Your Kids," and "Get Revenge: Live Long Enough to be a Problem to Your Children." What the prophets described about family relationships in the terminal era was not pretty. Imagine their making *"disobedient to parents"* a generational hallmark. This feature is prominent on the prophetic list the apostle Paul gave to his young disciple.

It probably goes without saying that if parents had their children under their moral restraints and physical control they could deal a significant blow to teenage drug and gang involvement, teenage promiscuity and pregnancy, and juvenile delinquency. As you read the hideous accounts of crimes by and against teens in the news, check where the kids were, what they were doing, what moral environment they were in when the crimes occurred and what time of night it was. You will find that teenagers—even preteens—are roaming the streets around the clock, out from under the umbrella of protection or authority of morally responsible parents.

Observe the relational dynamics between children and their parents and you will discover an epidemic of intimidated parents cowed by the rash, threatening and even brutal manner of their own flesh and blood. Feeding on rock, Heavy Metal or punk rock music which draws teenagers into an anarchistic subculture, teenagers have taken on the symbols of violent independence. Why else would they wear symbols of darkness (all black clothing), bondage (leather and chains) and brutality (metal spikes and studs) as teen fashion?

The increasing filial anarchy of the American home has become so acute that the head of MTV (the rock music cable TV channel) boasts, "We *own* the ninth graders of America." At the 1989 MTV music awards, groups visibly zoned out on drugs glorified illicit sex, preached contempt for parents and portrayed unrestrained hedonism. Actress-singer Cher paraded and gyrated her bare buttocks into the audience. Other top performers pranced in near-nudity, stroked their genitals and simulated sexual intercourse in dance routines. Many sneered at and debunked symbols of authority.

The kids loved it.

Even more frightening, our society is increasingly institutionalizing the "rights" of children to disobey. We live in a world in which your daughter can get pregnant and have an abortion without any legal obligation to tell you or get your consent. In many states the school officials, health officials and law enforcement institutions will all defend, protect and facilitate your teenager's "right" to operate without parental intervention in this matter. I attended a conference in which a speaker for the Center for Population Options praised the day in which free condoms *in school colors* would be provided at all public schools, thus providing your kids access to "safe" sex without your knowledge or approval.

11. Treachery Begins at Home

In two other prophetic warnings both Paul and Jesus describe a plague of trust-breaking in the end-time society. The writer-physician Luke carefully records a prophetic speech given by Jesus in which He portrays this bonanza of betrayal as striking at the heart of all human relationships, the family:

> You will be betrayed by parents, brothers, relatives, and friends, and they will put some of you to death.[13]

This verse raced through my mind as I read the follow-up to the massacre at Tienanmen Square in Beijing, Peoples Republic of China. Government officials, after lying to the national and international press about the nature and extent of the violence (in the face of press videotape releases to the contrary), sought to find student leaders of the protest for imprisonment and public execution.

They were often frustrated in their attempts by loyal fellow-protestors who hid them or helped them escape from the country. Many of those discovered and captured were aided *by family members who betrayed their whereabouts.*

The international sweep of the communist doctrine

and system which places loyalty to the state above family loyalties has made this phenomenon more widespread and common today than at any time in human history.

Should an oppressive, totalitarian, international, computer-coordinated regime assume global power and demand loyalty to The Glorious Leader or to The State, patterns of family loyalty will already have been broken. No longer will the expression "Blood is thicker than water" describe family bonds. Iron is thicker than both.

Treason Above Reason

While Jesus put betrayal in the context of close human relationships, both His and Paul's prophecies generalize it to cultural proportions in other places. "Treacherous" is on Paul's 2 Timothy list of warning signs. The word he uses appears three times in the Bible, translated "traitor" two times and "betrayer" the third.[14]

A person who expresses treacherous character is marked by two patterns of behavior. First, he will say anything, give his word, sign a contract, make an oath or swear on a stack of Bibles only to violate his commitment freely and without conscience whenever it serves his purposes to do so. Not only is his "word not his bond," he will allow himself to be bonded to no one. To do so would violate the high value he places on being in control of others and keeping his options open.

Secondly, he will actually premeditate the preparation and signing of contracts, agreements or truces *intending in advance to break them* in order to exploit the integrity of the other signatories.

This was a favorite *modus operandi* of Adolf Hitler. Throughout the stages of international diplomacy which led to World War II, Hitler signed accords, agreements, mutual defense pacts, truces and treaties with one hand, while with the other he prepared to break those commitments or go to war against the unsuspecting other parties.

Hitler signed an agreement with Great Britain's Prime Minister Neville Chamberlain at Munich, which Parliament ratified and Chamberlain announced would result in "peace for our time." On July 19, 1940, after the fall of France, *Der Fuhrer* made a speech in which he offered to make peace with Great Britain. "I can see no reason why this war must go on," he said. What the public did not know was that three days before his "peace speech" he had announced to his commanders, "I have decided to prepare a landing operation against England."[15]

In 1988 this same M.O. was used by one of America's largest corporations to exploit believers in Jesus Christ.

Universal Betrayal

Having already gone into the production of a movie under the working title *The Passion,* Universal Pictures prepared to launch a film eventually given the title of the novel on which it was based, *The Last Temptation of Christ.*

MCA/Universal, the biggest studio in the business, clearly expected Christians to be upset about the film. Years earlier Paramount had rejected the project by Martin Scorsese because it was too controversial to handle. So Universal board chairman, Tom Pollock, asked Tim Penland, a Christian believer who had experience marketing moral Hollywood films to the Christian community, to be a paid consultant to Universal.

Receiving a guarantee in writing that the film would be "faith affirming," that it would portray Jesus Christ "as sinless, as deity, and as the savior of mankind," and that the studio wanted to "build bridges to the Christian community," Penland accepted the position. After Penland had served the studio for months and top Christian leaders across the nation had agreed in good faith to attend a pre-screening of the movie to give input "far in advance of the release of the film," it was discovered that the whole plan was a betrayal.[16]

News leaked to the press that Scorsese and Universal had hired Penland to "shepherd the film past the protests of religionists." It became clear that the studio had no intention of following through with its scheduled screening for Christian leaders. Furthermore, it became clear that Universal had intended all along to exploit the controversy and its timing to swell the earnings at the box office.

Despite 25,000 protestors demonstrating outside Universal's headquarters and millions of letters and phone calls asking the company not to release a film which portrayed Jesus as a bedeviled, sex-crazed, seizure-ridden person, Universal pursued its intended objectives without restraint or apology.

This is just one high-level example of an increasingly common pattern of betrayal, breach of contracts and broken commitments.

12. Deception

This epidemic of cunning agreement-breaking provides a backdrop for humorist Andy Rooney's speculation that at any point in time half of America is in court suing the other half. After all, litigation results when one party seeks to *deceive* another.

Funny, isn't it, that widespread *deception* was another of the prophets' identifying marks of the end age: "Evil men and impostors will go from bad to worse, *deceiving and being deceived* [emphasis added]."[17]

Take all objective, absolute definitions of morality out of Western World ethics. Put in an international, political philosophy and doctrine which glorifies deception, contract-breaking and duplicity if it advances the "cause of the revolution" or the "interests of the state." The result? Global trust is at an all-time low.

When it comes to bad guys, we have a glut; the supply surely is surpassing the demand.

While going through religious motions, the last generation will deny the power behind its faith.

8

Fizzled Fission

"There will be terrible times in the last days. People will be lovers of themselves, lovers of money, boastful, proud, abusive, disobedient to their parents, **ungrateful, unholy,** without love, **unforgiving,** slanderous, **without self-control,** brutal, not lovers of the good, treacherous, rash, conceited, lovers of pleasure rather than lovers of God — **having a form of godliness but denying its power.** Have nothing to do with them."

Paul
2 Timothy 3:1-5

☐   ☐   ☐

I hadn't come thousands of miles from my home country into the tall forest jungles of South America for nothing. My journey had taken me on a series of successively smaller aircraft until a single-engine Piper with pontoons had delivered me to the jungle river. After a half-day ride on a river boat, I found myself in a clearing, seventy-five miles from the nearest unpaved road and very, very close to nowhere. If this wasn't the end of the world, it certainly lay down the trail a mile or two!

I had been asked to speak to an annual "field conference" of the missionaries who faithfully worked the mountains and jungles of that part of the world, seeking to introduce the nationals to the person and message of Jesus Christ. I had launched the week with two days of talks I felt would be inspirational.

I was wrong. My messages were going over like a concrete blimp.

Some of the missionaries, fine people, mind you, were sitting through the sessions with "come-on-I-dare-you-to-bless-me" looks on their faces. Others had pleasant enough countenances but seemingly little spiritual warmth behind their smiles.

In addition, I was sensing that all was not wonderful in paradise. Sitting in on an afternoon strategy session, I observed that defeatism was rampant. One burned-out and bummed-out missionary was recommending that the mission close one of its major structures. I learned that two of the three wives living on one remote compound were barely speaking to each other and had not darkened each others' doors for more than two years. Furthermore, I overheard family members at each others' throats through the thin walls of the jungle house where I was staying. Communication was at an all-time low.

I happen to believe that a vital faith is supposed to deal with situations exactly like this, so I took aggressive action. I called the U. S. and field leaders of the mission together for an evening powwow and shared my feelings.

"Men," I began, "nothing is happening here. The

spiritual climate is as cold as the Klondike. I don't feel there is any use proceeding with the conference until we can get some spiritual solutions. I suggest we suspend all programming for the conference and structure an open-ended prayer time until the God of heaven meets us. When He does, I'm willing to carry on."

We talked until late in the evening about the problems faced by the missionaries, about our spiritual concerns for them, and about what we would like to see God do, if He would answer our prayers and do something. We went to our knees and prayed until the evening was far gone.

Reach Out and Touch Someone

The next morning at the scheduled time for the session, we met in a primitive, screened-in, broad-board building plotted between the tropical palms and banana trees. The mission honcho announced that we were changing the schedule to permit a time for concentrated prayer. I gave a short devotional on the Holy Spirit and interpersonal relationships and announced we would go to prayer — first with silent prayers of confession.

Shortly into that time of silent prayer a hush fell over the room. The usual shuffling of feet, hacking, coughing and rustling of papers and books ceased as if throttled by some cosmic restrainer. The silence was deafening for first five, then ten minutes. Then I began hearing quiet sniffling.

I peeked.

All over the room people were weeping. Tears were streaming down the faces of men and women. Tears brought on sniffles. Sniffles brought out hankies. Hankies were everywhere. A few sobbed quietly.

I breathed a sigh of relief and joy and closed my eyes again. A strange, heavy burden I had been carrying dematerialized and lifted off my shoulders.

After a while I announced, "If anyone would like to express his prayer of confession audibly, he may feel comfortable doing so now."

Pause.

The handsome, well-built six-footer who headed the jungle home in which I was a guest rose to his feet and cried out in brokenness, "Oh God, forgive me. I've been a wretch to my wife and children!" He blubbered audibly and sat down.

The silence in the room increased a number of minus decibels.

Long pause.

A lady rose to her feet. She was one of the miffed matrons who had not been in the home of the other wife for years. "Oh Lord," she languished, "forgive me for my jealousy of Susan. I have envied her talent and so many other things about her. Please forgive me!" Weeping, she sat down.

This went on. Confession of bitterness. Confession of impure, lustful thinking. Confession of discouragement and negativism. Confession of spiritual coldness. Tear ducts flowed like artesian wells.

When the free confessions ceased, I suggested we sing. Sing we did.

Heaven Came Down

I can't imagine thirty voices blended in more angelic harmony. Spontaneous old-time hymns of praise to God.

Moving contemporary expressions of intimacy with Christ. All in harmonic *a cappella*. The fusion of human spirits melted into one grand symphonic movement.

The declaration of my wristwatch knocked me cold. We had been doing this for close to four hours. It was past time for lunch. The hours had passed like milliseconds.

I suggested that everybody hug somebody on the way to lunch. Nobody headed for lunch. The room turned into tag-team hugging matches. The two estranged wives embraced and wept. The handsome six-footer tenderly held his petite wife as tears splashed off their cheeks onto each other. Crusty old missionary warriors cast off their machismo and engaged in bone-crushing loveholds.

One burly veteran approached a young executive from the Florida home office. "Bob," he began, "I've hated you. I've resented everything coming from you and from the office. But it's been wrong. Please forgive me." As he spoke that last line, he grabbed the exec around the waist and hoisted him off the floor about six inches in an *abrazo* of restoration.

Divine power in a Peruvian rain forest!

Dealing From the Ideal

What purpose is religion supposed to serve anyway? Wouldn't it seem that one's faith in a supreme being would generate a source of inspiration, good will, love and charity? Doesn't it make sense that a body of believers would become, through shared communion with deity and acknowledgment of common transgression, more like an organ*ism* than an organ*ization*? Wouldn't it seem normative that sharing the atonement for human sins that comes from faith would be a great leveler of all mankind, turning it into a brotherhood and sisterhood of humanity? Shouldn't truth, justice, purity and integrity flow out of the motivations and values instilled by a benevolent divine donor in His followers?

So it would seem. But rarely is it true.

My jungle ecstasy has been recaptured on other occasions in variant forms to varying degrees. When it is, I feel that this is true religion and not the plastic, self-righteous, political and social hocus-pocus that exploits the sacred to gain advantage over the profane.

Is it not true religion that makes *homo sapiens* into a human family? Is it not the demise of faith which causes the fabric of human bonding to rot? I believe it is. The "decline of religion" was, after all, one of the five factors cited by Gibbons in the fall of Rome.

Thus, we come to the last — and I believe the most terrifying — of all prophetic pictures of the end-time era: *perverse religion*. The apostle Paul's list of end-time indicators includes five characteristics describing a dramatic decline of religion in the last generation.

13. No Thanks!

It seems that a natural result of faith would be *gratitude* for the blessings which each of us receives from the divine hand. I would think that religion would stir thankfulness in the heart of man, rather than a fist-shaking in the face of God for every little thing that is not to our liking. But not so. The apostle Paul describes last-generation people as chronic ingrates.

I love the story of the hayseed who stops for lunch at the big city restaurant while in town to purchase supplies for farm and family. A quartet of smart-mouthed teenagers jammed in a nearby booth heap ridicule on him for his bib overalls, straw hat and the weed stickers in his socks. When he bows for prayer over the warm meal just served him, the juveniles laugh uproariously and taunt, "Hey, Bumpkin, everybody where you come from do that?"

After a sufficient enough pause to clear his mouth of the first bite of food, the farmer responds, "Nope. The pigs don't."

The prophet declares this final generation of people to be *"unthankful."*[1] He chooses a word which denotes "without a gracious or grateful response." This swine-like attribute apparently is quite offensive to God. Paul says that a key reason all of mankind stands condemned before God is that "although they knew God, they neither glorified Him as God *nor gave thanks to Him* [emphasis added]."[2]

The self-loving, compassionless, arrogant, slanderous people described earlier surely do not possess the character quality which motivated Farmer John to bow before his meal. These people, rather than singing "Count your blessings, name them one by one," curse the absence of blessings they feel they deserve.

And, strangely, some of this ingratitude is being fed by religions. In pop culture, where religious fads come and go like Pacific tides, a number of religious philosophies work against gratitude. Terry Cole Whittaker, the San Diego, California, leader of a TV-based religious system, distributed bumper stickers among her followers proclaiming, "Prosperity: Your Divine Right." I presume that if you are receiving anything less from life than "prosperity," you have a basis for cursing God.

Honor Thyself

Now add the man-centered religions of the day which exalt human beings as gods or gods-in-the-making and you arrive at a world view which creates ingrates by spontaneous combustion. Consider the ungrateful attitude displayed in the teachings of L. L. Whyte, philosopher and stage setter for the New Age Movement:

> It has long been held that whoever denies God asserts his own divinity. In dropping God, man recovers himself. It is about time that God be put in his place, that is, in man, and no nonsense about it.[3]

Werner Erhard, founder of EST and Forum, spouts the doctrine of one of his mentors, Swami Muktananda:

> Kneel to your own self. Honor and worship your own being. God dwells within you as You![4]

This not-so-subtle doctrine of ingratitude underlies even the preaching and teaching of many Christian ministers, especially those in the "prosperity school." It is not at all uncommon to hear ministers on Christian TV networks declaring that the absence of health, wealth and power indicates either (1) a sin problem or (2) lack of faith. The premise is that the "King's kids" deserve the best this life has to offer and can have it if they claim it. Many schooled in this system are embittered because God didn't deliver what was "rightfully theirs" as children of God—a far cry from the message of the children's song, "Be thankful for the good things that you've got . . ."

14. Unholy Mackerel!

"Is nothing sacred?" is the cry of those offended by impiety. The last time span will be an *unholy* era, according to the prophets. The Greek word designating this characteristic describes a generation devoid of any respect for those things which are sacred, hallowed, sanctified or consecrated. The line between the sacred and the profane is so blurred that it's practically non-existent.

The TV show *Saturday Night Live* regularly parodies God, Jesus, prayer, the Bible, salvation, Spirit-filling and other things divine and sacred. The "Church Lady" is a weird, out-of-touch, self-righteous human being who condemns the idea of "sin" while showing sinful urges herself. The "Thumper Family" (as in "Bible thumper") is ridiculed for praying on its knees and pursuing distinctly Christian values. Billy Graham is portrayed as a singing telegram delivery boy calling on an unmarried couple living together to sing a telegram denouncing them as fornicators (sneer) "living in *sin.*"

The phrase "born again" has been corrupted by the media to include everything from gaining a new hair color to having an ecstatic sexual experience. In Washington, D. C., men wearing buttons declaring "Born Again Gay" lobby congressmen.

In San Bernardino, California, the pastor of a new gay church delivers messages proclaiming that David and Jonathan and Jesus and John had gay relationships. Cartoonists show a car with two bumper stickers: "Jesus Saves" and "Jim and Tammy Spend."

The judge on *Night Court* hangs a basketball hoop on a life-sized Calvary cross and shoots baskets into it. Madonna (note the stage name) shoots a sexually suggestive music video ("Like a Prayer") in a church wearing a cross around her neck and fondling the statue of a saint. *Hustler* magazine runs a photo feature showing nudes nailed to crosses, crowns of thorns and all. Among the pieces of art shown at a prominent Atlanta gallery and endowed by the National Academy of Art is a picture of Jesus Christ in a sea of urine dubbed by the artist "The Piss Christ."

In Miami, Florida, a Christian church had to close its "always open" prayer chapel because teenagers from the nearby high school were using it like a brothel. In Great Britain gays dress up like nuns to disrupt Christian music concerts. All over the world occultists vandalize churches and use the cross in sexual orgies and bloody sacrificial rituals. In the Marxist-socialist world, faith in a supreme being is debunked, church-goers persecuted and theism ridiculed and banned from halls of learning.

There's more, much more, but you get the point. The end-time generation is damnably *unholy*. End-time religion does not define and defend the sacred; it profanes it and sanctifies the debased.

15. Don't Get Mad, Get Even

Religions, even forms not rooted in Judeo-Christian values, commonly have methods for gaining atonement (forgiveness for earthly wrongdoing). Whether it is the casting of a child into the burning jowls of Moloch or engaging in ritual incantations and self-torture, most religions believe appeasement and forgiveness must be attained.

In the best interests of human relationships and human brotherly love, the forgiveness of others is often valued highly by religion. Moving scenes in the film *The Mission* illustrate the glorious attainment of forgiveness. In *Les Miserables,* the redemptive forgiveness of the priest and of Jean Valjean, the lead character, has thrilled audiences by the millions.

But the prophets indicate that in the time just preceding the end, forgiveness will *not* be an attribute of human society. What I would consider to be a primary benefit of religion, the encouragement of forgiving and forgetting, will not be in ascendance. In fact, the picture is that even religion will be captivated by unforgiving vengefulness.

When the prophet calls the epoch "unforgiving," he is describing a character weakness marked by an *unwillingness to spend or be spent to make amends*. The possessor of this trait is absolutely implacable, unable to be appeased. He burns with bitter vengeance and is motivated to retribution regardless of the efforts of another to reconcile. It is Rambo bent on destroying all who cross him. It is Dirty Harry wanting the bad guys to "make his day."

In the real world it is an Ayatollah Khomeini breathing terrorist vengeance on any who don't fit his grid. Bomb a loaded commercial aircraft filled with innocents. Atomize a Marine barracks. Machine gun an embassy or a restaurant. All is justified in the name of retribution, *religious* retribution.

Even in conservative Christianity one evangelical leader rushes to Ted Koppel's *Nightline* program to rat on the deeds of another evangelical leader, and former employees of fallen televangelists squeal on their mentors in bursts of "I'll-get-you-before-you-get-me" retaliation.

This is an era in which religions, with all their noble teachings of redemption, cannot restrain the tidal wave of vengeance. All the king's horses and all the king's men can't put forgiveness together again.

16. Who Put the Imp in Impulses?

Dr. Armand M. Nicholi, II is a psychiatrist on the faculty of Harvard Medical School and the staff of Massachusetts General Hospital. Dr. Nicholi is a student of behavioral trends in America, particularly those involving the family. In lectures and articles he describes an alarming condition in America he calls "lack of impulse control":

> Society seems to have given up on its traditional civilizing task of controlling aggressive and sexual impulses. The deep moral confusion we have observed over the past decade seems to have lifted all restraint. During the past ten years, I have noticed a marked change in the type of problems that people bring to a psychiatrist. Previously, a great many came because of their inability to express impulses and feelings. Today, the majority come because of an inability to *control* their impulses.[5]

Isn't it interesting that New Testament prophetic literature portrays the end-time epoch as *"without self-control."* Without getting highly statistical here, let me survey some of the dynamics in a society lacking impulse control:

Lack of control of aggressive impulses:

> *Assault and battery*
> *Child abuse*
> *Spouse battering*
> *Gang violence*
> *Armed robbery*
> *Rape*
> *Sadomasochism*
> *Suicide*

Lack of control of sexual impulses:

> *Rape*
> *Sexual addiction*
> *Pornography*
> *Prostitution*
> *Homosexuality*
> *Lesbianism*
> *Bestiality*
> *Sadomasochism*
> *Child molesting*
> *Incest*

Kiddie porn
Adultery
Teenage pregnancy
AIDS and other sexually transmitted diseases

Lack of control of non-sexual appetites:

Gluttony
Obesity
Alcoholism
Smoking
Substance abuse
Greed and material self-indulgence
Vainglory
Theft
Occult practices
Divorce

There are more than thirty items in the above three lists. Let me ask *you*: How many of those dynamics have radically increased during the past fifty years? How many are more common in your own personal experience than they were when you were a child?

I think I can clinch this point by citing evidence for items from the above list which I view as most in violation of common human decency.

Ad Nauseam

The lid has been on the world of "S/M," sado-masochism, until the last decade or so. Sadomasochists derive sexual delight from inflicting and/or experiencing pain. Imagine being so twisted in one's motivations and impulses that pain becomes pleasure and inflicting it on another becomes fulfilling. But this sexual aberration has now become so acceptable that it has been featured on made-for-TV movies and sitcoms. Our teenage children, who I'm sure do not all realize what their clothing signifies, spend hundreds of dollars on black leather bondage boots, spiked heels, studded leather gloves and wristbands and other paraphernalia that has moved from the S/M underground to the fashion pages of their teen magazines.

A leading department store in a major U. S. city decorated its windows in S/M themes. Women's magazines have produced full fashion layouts in which models are clothed in S/M attire. Shops openly sell leather whips, erotic clothing featuring leather, chains and spikes, and elaborate devices of torture. A significant percentage of pornographic literature is devoted to describing and showing individuals in a mixture of erotica and excruciation. One of my graduate school professors nearly burned down a motel in the practice of his masochism. And the San Francisco police department is documenting an increased number of *deaths* each year from S/M sexual experiences — torment gone to the limit.

If I am revulsed at the thought of torturing myself or others for fulfillment, I am more sickened at the thought of man and animal engaging in sexual acts, a practice so damnable that the Old Testament Law sentenced both man and animal to death,[6] and proclaimed that any nation which allowed such practices *even by visitors or aliens* would "vomit out its inhabitants."[7]

Yet bestiality is increasingly common especially in the burgeoning homosexual community. One book reports that one-fifth of all homosexuals admitted to having sexual contact with animals.[8] Charles Shively, a prominent homosexual, wrote an article for the gay *Fag Rag* entitled, "Bestiality as an Act of Revolution." *The Gay Report,* a widely read and lauded book in the homosexual community, reports positive testimonials with no apparent shame and no adverse comments from those having sex with a variety of animals.[9]

Likewise, it is absolutely inconceivable to me that an adult would have sexual urges so out of control that he would violate the innocence of a defenseless child. Research shows how utterly naive I am. I mentioned earlier that there are more than 350 titles of child pornography in distribution feeding a growing appetite for kiddie porn.

Driven to this abominable lust by child porn, adults molest, procure, kidnap and seduce children into sex acts by the hundreds of thousands each year. Father Ritter reports that "people can openly ask for films or magazines showing a six-year-old child having sex with another six-year-old or an adult."[10]

Add to this fact that as many as forty million (one in six) Americans have been sexually abused in childhood.[11] Compound this with the observation that most child molestation is perpetrated by *family members* (incest) or *close family friends,* and it is regurgitation time.

As someone keenly observed, "If God doesn't rain judgment on much of modern America, He will owe an apology to Sodom and Gomorrah."

17. Amid Flotsam and Jetsam

Where is religion in restraining this flood of spiritual excrement? Helplessly adrift in the same moral effluent.

New Age religion destroys all distinctions between right and wrong by making good and evil one. Mainline Protestant denominations are ordaining gay and lesbian ministers while an entire movement of homosexual and lesbian priests and nuns has arisen in the Roman Catholic Church. The "Teen Sex Survey in the Evangelical Church," a study of the moral practices of teenagers in eight of the most conservative, Bible-believing denominations in America, revealed that 43 percent of these churched teens had sex by age eighteen.[12] This was in churches as "straight arrow" as the Salvation Army, Church of the Nazarene, Missouri Synod Lutheran and Grace Brethren.

Once again, "Where is religion in salting the society with its moral and spiritual influence?" Precisely where the New Testament prophets declared it would be: *"Possessing all the external shapes and forms of being God-fearing people but running their lives in abject poverty of any spiritual power. Have absolutely nothing to do with these people!"*[13]

Here the apostle Paul gave a perfect, prophetic picture of American religion — Catholic, Protestant and Jewish. All three operate like a dreamy fifteen-year-old fantasizing about getting his driver's license. He sits in Dad's car going through all the motions of driving with the engine turned off.

Embarrassingly for me, this predictive condemnation was directed primarily at *Christians*. We are in sorry shape. We let our government keep "In God We Trust" on our coinage and worship the silver rather than the Savior. Even the 82.5 million of us who profess to have had a revolutionary and life-changing encounter with Jesus Christ can't keep our own kids from getting pregnant or zoned out on crack, much less prevent or retard the spiritual and moral rot of our own communities like any good "salt" should do.

The prophet said the end-time era, while going through religious motions, would *"deny the power"* behind its faith. The word he used for power is the word from which we get *dynamite*. So rare is it in this generation to see the explosive power of living faith that you may not, in your lifetime, ever have witnessed *anything close* to the experience in the Peruvian jungle I described at the outset of this chapter. You probably cannot postulate what pours out when Power presses His penetrating presence onto the perverse priorities of people pretending to pursue His plan.

Friend, until you have experienced the *fission* which blows apart your pride and self-sufficiency and the *fusion* which "spot welds" your spirit to that of God's and your fellow-man's, *life has escaped you.* Why, without that discovery, these eight grim chapters could be mistakenly perceived to be terminal. If that has been your conclusion, you don't understand this power.

Depending on what's done with it, the force within a nuclear substance the size of an apple can atomize a city or energize it. I'm sorry that the world of religion—even Christianity—has had *fizzled fission.* I can't wait to describe for you the "end-time energizing" that the prophets foretold.

Miss it and you miss the most dramatic pageant in the history of the universe—the destructive power of a billion Hiroshimas and the constructive force of a trillion reactors all converging on a seven-year epoch which could begin at any time.

Lucifer's "Master Strategy"
for our generation.

9

Satan's Half-Century Plan

"I have great hopes that we shall learn in due time how to emotionalize and mythologize their science to such an extent that what is, in effect, a belief in us (though not under that name) will creep in while the human mind remains closed to belief in the Enemy."

Screwtape to Wormwood
The Screwtape Letters
C. S. Lewis

☐ ☐ ☐

It's a meeting of the Demonic High Council at the Lower Regions Headquarters near where the River Styx flows into the Lake of Fire. The week-long, high-level briefing session is proceeding with Satan presiding over the High Council. The date is **Friday, October 13, 1947.** Satan speaks.

"Brothers and sisters of the darkness, I have called this meeting to plan our Western World strategy for the next fifty years. Now that the so-called Allied Nations have emerged victorious on the battlefields over our favorite son, Adolf Hitler, and many of our brothers, we must design a plan to assure that this result does not become a victory in the *soulish* dimension!

"By the way, wasn't the war a spectacular time for all of us?"

[Wild applause, shouted expletives and cheers.]

"Not bad to be able to orchestrate this twice in thirty years, huh?"

[More rounds of cheering, toasting of glasses of ale and applause.]

"Without a doubt this tops all our previous efforts in modern Europe! Particularly outstanding was the unleashing of uncontrolled violence, hatred, torture, misery and bloodshed. Our successes will remain in the memories of the race for generations. It was beautiful.

"My congratulations to you, Theron, for your oversight of the European theatre for the past four millennia. You surely did yourself proud on this one!"

[Cheers and applause.]

"And, Domni, your management of the Chosen People Detail [laughter] was nothing less than a 'flaming success!' [More laughter.] I'll never forget the looks on the faces of the 'conquerors' as they walked among the ovens at Dachau. That was worth the whole effort."

For a scriptural basis for the fictional scenario presented in this chapter, see Appendix A, "Biblical Background for Satan's 'Half-Century Plan.' "

[Wild cheers and congratulatory handshakes all around.]

"Enough of the celebrating and back-patting. I have been thinking ahead. Today I would like to present my plan for the Western nations for the next half-century. Give your attention to the psychic monitor. Here is an outline of the plan in simplified terms."

Murmuring, growling demons wriggle in their chairs to get comfortable and close their eyes as they enter a low-level trance. Satan mutters some unintelligible utterances, and images begin to appear in the minds of the High Council members. An outline flashes on and off the psyches of the unclean spirits. Interspersed with outline points are images of what each outline principle might look like in execution.

The Half-Century Plan

Lucifer, his massive body dwarfing the podium, begins reading the outline and making explanatory comments on each point:

"First of all, POLITICALLY, we will let the nations pursue their so-called 'democratic ideals.' They will believe that this war was the end of all such wars [chuckles from the audience], and we can exploit this notion. While democracies are not so easily controlled as totalitarian systems, we *can* control them. We direct our efforts to breaking down the so-called 'moral consensus' and people eventually vote in our programs without our having to force them onto them through terror and tyranny. Democracies are no resistance to us unless the values of the voting majority are the values of that archfiend Jehovah.

"Second, in the ECONOMIC AREA, we have the nations right where we want them. They are all debt-ridden from war expenditures and the memory of the Great Depression is still fresh in their minds. The masses will almost instinctively become obsessed with the value of money, of material things and of 'financial security.' I love it. This obsession will provide a permanent distraction from spiritual pursuits which the #*!! enemy is always trying to promote.

"Unless I have read the cards wrong, I predict that ADVANCING TECHNOLOGY will get to the place where the money system will be completely systematized and unified for efficiency's sake. When it is, we will gain control over it and thereby control the ability of every person and structure on earth to make financial transactions of the simplest kind. Then the earthlings will be eating out of our hands.

"INTELLECTUALLY we'll use pride as our main strategy. Among the Allies the United States will be most proud of its prowess not only in the rapid creation of its war machine but in the scientific and technological achievements which made the war effort a success. Possessing the bomb will be a heady experience for the U. S. We can use this to reinforce the idea that God, damn Him, is a useless and obsolete entity for people who are so intelligent and self-sufficient, who possess an instrument of terror and who have science under their control.

"SOCIALLY, the absence of a unifying cause, such as the war effort, will erode social cohesion. This will make it a great time to exploit interclass, interracial and interethnic hatreds. Divide! Divide! Divide! Promote every possible variation of prejudice, suspicion, contempt and discrimination. If we can sell societies on the supremacy of *individual* rights, *individual* freedoms and *self* aggrandizement, we will have it made.

"And council members, curse you, hear what I say! A

very major enemy is, and I hate the phrase, the 'traditional family.' 'Traditional' means everything we despise! It
means marriage. It means commitment and fidelity of
mates. If the traditional family succeeds, all of our 'sexual
freedom' stratagems are useless: adultery, pornography,
homosexuality, lesbianism, incest and the more fun types.

"So don't forget this! Repeat after me: 'Damn the
family! Damn the family! Damn the family!' "

Satan's eyes burn like hot coals and his face contorts
into a tight sneer. The fiends arouse temporarily from their
psychic monitoring. The hall reverberates with the chants
of the hordes. Chandeliers rattle. Cracks appear in the
plaster. Their eyes glow and their fangs glisten as they
chant for what seems like hours before the intonations
wane.

Leathery eyelids close and bodies assume a relaxed
position once again. Images again appear on the psychic
screens of the vile spirits.

Satan resumes his briefing, shifting his position a bit.
The fire in his eyes has darkened to embers.

"Now I want to talk to you about THE ARTS. I am not
at all pleased with what you have been doing in this area.
In art and music, particularly, we still have this damnable,
goody-goody God stuff! I am sick of great musical works
being dedicated to the glory of Jesus [sneers] and art that
features, of all things, Bible stories. We have been through
four to six hundred years of this garbage. Handel, Renais-
sance paintings, Michelangelo, Da Vinci, the Sistine
Chapel, Gothic cathedrals. I *puke* at the thought.

"Damn you all, I will not put up with the enemy's
predominance in the arts anymore, do you hear?"

Satan pounds the podium with such force that the imprint of his fist is embedded in it. His breath is steam-like. The ghouls gasp and wheeze at the shock and then settle back to the psychic monitor again.

Capturing the Electronic Village

"These next fifty years will be *ours* in the arts. I predict this new invention called 'television' will be our primary weapon. We will also use films. Other technologies will make the entire world an *electronic village* which we can control.

"If we play it right, I foresee the day when the masses will relish violence in films, on television and, subsequently, in real life. They will pay billions to see blood spilled, people disemboweled and innocents tortured and dismembered. I dream of the day when even kids, socialized by the electronic media, will wear the symbols of death and violence and carry instruments of torture and death to *elementary* schools. I envision a day in which electronic means will enable every individual to view every type of sexual scene — visions with such force that even *one view* will leave the looker forever altered in our direction. This will make sexual addiction a cinch."

The accumulated personifications of slime stir in their chairs, moved by the exciting prospect of the vision. They have never heard anything like this before. Could such glorious things be possible?

The dragon continues.

"Music will be as powerful as television. Everyone in the race listens to some kind of music. We will gradually and subtly slip more and more of our thinking into popular songs. First, we will do it by double entendre. As people grow more accepting of this, we will become more explicit. We will ultimately proclaim unbridled sex, promote hatred and violence, and exalt contempt for all authority including that of the enemy. Gradually, we will instruct listeners at the subliminal level to adore all that we espouse.

"If we are successful, I foresee the day when a subculture of musicians will lead an entire generation of youth into everything we advocate. Our musicians will be their role models and folk heroes. As the melodies and instrumentations distract and bypass their rational resistances, the lyrics and images created by our servant performers will enslave their souls. We will possess them, and they will honor us. They will sing praises to us. They will worship us. They will be *ours*. We will enslave them by proclaiming *freedom* until all boundaries to thought and behavior have been destroyed. It takes only one generation to assure victory. *We will prevail!*"

As if jolted to their feet by some high-voltage shock, the Demonic High Council members burst onto their feet in a deafening, standing ovation. Guttural grunts, ear-shattering screeches and the deafening slap-slapping of demon wings make the noise level unbearable. But they don't seem to mind. Master Lucifer's words have intoxicating power.

Gradually the cacophony of other-worldly sounds subsides. The Prince of Darkness approaches his last point, swelled to half-again his size with pride from the ovation.

Unholy Trinity

"High Council, I have saved the best part of this strategy for the last. After all of these millennia being frustrated by the religion of the hideous heavenly host and by its impact on the race, I have come up with a *devilish* plan. Heh, heh! Toward the end of this fifty-year plan we will begin revealing *our own SUBSTITUTE FOR CHRISTIANITY*. Maybe we can call it *Curse*tianity!"

[Guffaws.]

"I will send *my* 'only begotten son' to earth. After he has reached maturity in the early twenty-first century, he will preach love and peace until he has solidified his power. He will do mighty miracles to prove his claim to be the 'savior of the world' and will unite all the nations of the world into one political and religious entity. In so doing, he will steal the power and glory from Christ. In reality, everything he does will be anti-Christ.

"In the meantime, with the rank and file of the army of the Nazarene neutralized by the daily, repetitive bombardment of our messages from the intellectual world and from electronic media, we can create a party atmosphere of pleasure seeking. Even the Christians will be so involved in having a good time—in their puritanical style, of course—they will be unwilling to take up arms against us.

"In the rest of the world, millions will seek their thrills in drunkenness and hallucinogenic drugs. This is fabulous! With drug addiction removing the guard from their human spirits, they will be defenseless against our attempts to influence and possess them. I believe we can so brainwash one whole generation of people on earth that they will be totally oblivious to the impending disaster which awaits them.

"But here is the best part. [The demons are on the edges of their seats, still concentrating on the monitor.] After my own 'Son of God' is operating, I plan to send into the world my own spirit in the form of a great, prophetic oracle. *Voilà!* We will then have Satan the Father, Satan the Son and Satan the Unholy Spirit! If that doesn't dazzle you, I even plan to have my son slain and rise again from the dead. How about that? [The demons stir with excitement.] I expect this to be such a slick imitation of what Jehovah and the boys have going that even J. C.'s own troops won't be able to detect the con game if He doesn't tip them off to it.

"By then our own 'Messiah' will be in total control, and no one will dare stand against him! Comrades, if you join me in pursuing this plan, I believe that by the early part of the twenty-first century *we will have won the universal war!*"

To another thunderous, standing ovation Beelzebub folds up his notes. Eyes open as the transmissions of the psychic monitor cease. Demons raise clenched fists, give each other celebratory "high-three's" with their clawed hands and emit spontaneous, hiss-like cheers of "Hail Satan! Hail Satan! Hail Satan!" The devil leaves the podium, and the hideous creatures of the High Council file out bearing sadistic grins and murmuring praise for the master's "Half-Century Plan."

Forget the Red Longjohns

You may be one of the millions who do not believe in the existence of demons and the devil. Or you may consider the devil a comic creature with horns, a pitchfork and red longjohns.

If so, C. S. Lewis would consider you victimized by one of Satan's key strategies, described in a letter from Screwtape to Wormwood. Screwtape is an experienced, high-order demon in hell. The rookie demon, Wormwood, has been assigned a human "patient," and Screwtape is giving him counsel on strategy:

My dear Wormwood, I wonder you should ask me whether it is essential to keep the patient in ignorance of your own existence. That question, at least for the present phase of the struggle, has been answered for us by the High Command. Our policy for the moment is to conceal ourselves. Of course this has not always been so. We are really faced with a cruel dilemma. When the humans disbelieve in our existence we lose all the pleasing results of direct terrorism, and we make no magicians. On the other hand, when they believe in us, we cannot make them materialists and skeptics. At least, not yet. I have great hopes that we shall learn in due time how to emotionalize and mythologize their science to such an extent that what is, in effect, a belief in us (though not under that name) will creep in while the human mind remains closed to belief in the Enemy.[1]

Denying the existence of Satan is no compliment to mankind. It means that mankind has created and perpetrated the awesome evil of the centuries *all by himself,* unaided and unseduced by any occult beings. If that's your idea of an argument for human superiority, "No thanks!"

The fact is that both Old and New Testament biblical prophets affirm the existence, personality and activity of Lucifer and his hordes, even if experience and occultic phenomena didn't. Another fact is that most of the dimensions of the "Half-Century Plan" were drawn *directly from the prophetic visions* of the apostle John and other biblical prophets.

The imminence of the catastrophe on last generation people is so dramatic that Jesus Himself predicted it would be comparable only to the shock of the great flood on the people of Noah's day. Read it in Christ's own words:

No one knows about that day or hour, not even the angels in heaven or the Son, but only the Father. As it was in the days of Noah, so it will be at the coming of the Son of Man. For in the days before the flood, people were eating and drinking, marrying and giving in marriage, up to the day Noah entered into the ark; and they knew nothing about what would happen until the flood came and took them all away. That is how it will be at the com-

ing of the Son of Man. Two men will be in the field; one
will be taken and the other left. Two women will be grind-
ing with a hand mill; one will be taken and the other left.[2]

A few days ago, as I was writing the first part of this
chapter, a 7.1 earthquake ripped the San Francisco area,
dealing death to dozens, injury to more than 4,000 and
property destruction in the billions. The 60,000 fans
gathered in San Francisco's Candlestick Park for the
second baseball game of the World Series had no clue that
before the umpire could shout "Play ball!" the area would
receive $7 billion worth of devastation in *fifteen seconds.*
They and most of the residents of that area weren't
prepared for it, despite years of repeated warnings and
numerous previous quakes. This is precisely the picture
Jesus paints of the coming end-time disasters accompanied
by His return.

*Wait a minute, Poland. Where did the return of Jesus
get in here? I thought you were sketching the final destruction of the world in the final-chapter generation.*

Sorry if I slipped one in on you. I will show in a later
chapter that the end-time degeneration and the return of
Jesus are prophesied to occur in the same time period. For
now, tuck that away in your mind for future reference as I
wrap up the predictions regarding the catastrophic last
chapter of civilization. After that we'll discover the mar-
velous good news associated with it all.

Rock Around the Clock

Whether or not you buy the idea that slipping occult
messages into popular music was part of Lucifer's
worldwide Half-Century Plan, it has happened.

In my high school days, a Tennessean named Elvis
Presley angered parents by his sexually erotic pelvic move-

ments as he belted out songs, which, at their worst, were mildly suggestive. I think now most parents would choose Elvis fifty to one over the rock music artists of today. At least Elvis didn't exalt sex, death, gore and Satan.

Things have changed. In the early seventies a male singer named Alice Cooper pioneered a new kind of music he called "shock rock" in which he dressed in grotesque costumes and stabbed and dismembered dolls in simulations of violent acts. Cooper still tours with a spin-off version of his original group. The genre of music he performs is now dubbed "splatter rock" after the ultra-violent "slasher" films like *The Texas Chainsaw Massacre, Friday the Thirteenth* and *Nightmare on Elm Street*.

Rock music of one form or another (from soft hits all the way to Heavy Metal) is far and away the most popular music in America—consider the ratio of rock music radio stations to all other kinds of music stations. In the midst of the rock music craze, the mixing of music with sex, gore, death and the occult has become so common that there are whole categories of rock music pursuing these themes: Black Metal, Death Metal, Gloom Rock and Satan Rock.

Music groups of these types dress up like freak shows and feature the grossest kinds of violent images accompanied by hard-driving rock music. Performances feature skulls, blood, simulated slashings, mutilations and decapitations. Some performers gnaw on bones or drink blood as part of their acts. This is dark, evil, angry, hate-filled, rebellion-fed music. It features love for violence and gore.

Motley Crüe's "Too Fast for Love" boasts, "I'll either break her face or take down her legs, get my ways at will." In the movie *Predator* a few years ago, Genocide sang of a "heart ripped from the chest decapitated, a meal of vaginas and breasts.[3]

You may think these are isolated cases. Wrong. This type of music is a major movement in the youth culture of the Western World. And just how did this music turn this dark in less than a generation? The secret is to be found, I believe, in one other dominant theme of this music—the occult.

Creatures of the Cloven Hoof

Many performances of Death Metal, Black Metal, Gloom Rock and Satan Rock include occult images, satanic rites and references to magic. Written into the lyrics are glorifications of Satan and the occult. An acquaintance of mine who, before he gave his life to Jesus Christ, was a reporter covering the rock music scene, told me of being backstage before a major rock concert and observing the performers praying and dedicating their performance to Satan.

Satan and his cohorts are featured attractions in this form of "entertainment." Dominant fantasy themes of this music include black magic and Satan's underworld. A sampling of the names of the scores of Black Metal groups will make the point:[4]

Axe Witch	*Hellion*
Cryptic Slaughter	*Hell Star*
Coven	*Heretic*
Cloven Hoof	*Impaler*
Dark Angel	*Infernal Majesty*
Demon	*Omen*
Evil Dead	*Onslaught*
Grave Digger	*Possessed*
Grim Reaper	*Rigor Mortis*
Hallow's Eve	*Satan*
Helloween	*Sinner*
Hell Hammer	*Warlock*

While a few of the above groups are now defunct, their recordings are still being played across the land. Their mix of blood and guts, death and the occult is captured in the lyrics of a *Megadeath* song, "Good Mourning, Black Friday":

> Killer, intruder, homicidal man, If you see me coming, run as fast as you can. A bloodthirsty demon who's stalking the street, I hack up my victims like pieces of meat.[5]

The rock group *Possessed* proclaims:

> I drink the vomit of the priests, make love to the dying whore . . . . I am decreed by Lord Satan's fine evil to destroy what all mortals love most. Satan, my master incarnate, hail praise to my unholy host.[6]

Sales of the records, tapes, compact discs, T-shirts and other paraphernalia of these groups total in the billions of dollars. It is quite possible that if you have a teenaged devotee of hard rock music, he owns an album from one of these groups. He certainly has heard the music on one of the many "underground" radio stations, on the MTV cable channel or at the houses of his friends. The occult-glorifying messages being consumed by millions is working its way into your teen's subconscious mind.

Dr. Paul King, a child psychiatrist who treats disturbed teens at a Memphis, Tennessee, clinic, says the violent drug abusers he treats are "by and large into Heavy Metal. The music doesn't make them do it, but the lyrics become their philosophy."[7]

The Inverted Cross

Over and over I've heard people claim that one's *en-*

joyment of a particular style of music can be separated from any *expression* of the messages. But consider the following: Violent, occult-inspired crime has become the new wave of law-breaking America. "In the '60s, the cutting edge was drugs," says Washington journalist Larry Kahaner, author of *Cults That Kill,* a 1988 book which has become a helpful guide to law enforcement in understanding occult crime. "In the '70s, it was computer crime. In the '80s, it's terrorism. Occult crime is really the crime of the '90s."[8]

The exponential increase in occultic crime has created a demand among law enforcement agencies for the likes of detective Patrick Metoyer, a twenty-three-year-veteran of the Los Angeles Police Department. Metoyer is a bomb expert, watch commander for the criminal conspiracy section of the LAPD, and not one to go in for the "far out." But after being assigned to guard a witness for three months in the case of the Charles Manson murders, Metoyer began seeing the powers of cult leaders in tandem with the operations of those dabbling in Satanism. Now he has a presentation for law enforcement people that is so grisly even the toughest officers have difficulty believing such crimes could happen.

But happen they do. Murders in which the victim is decapitated so that the brains and eyes can be used in ritual sacrifices and potions before returning the mutilated head to the scene of the crime. Tortured and mutilated animals used in rituals for body parts and blood for drinking. A human left hand cut off a corpse to give the satanists the power of evil. A man in a sex act with a cadaver. I'm writing this in October, and the local animal shelter announced that it will not allow the adoption of black cats this Halloween month in fear they will be used for satanic rituals.

The interest by law enforcement in occultic crimes is so great that Larry Jones, president of Cult Crime Impact

Network and a lieutenant in the Boise, Idaho, police force, has created an informational newsletter which has 1,750 subscribers. Police have to be able to spot the telltale signs of a satanic crime to help in the crime's solution.[9]

When Jim Hardy and two of his friends beat to death their high school friend in Carl Junction, Missouri, they did so because "Satan had told them to." Hardy and his two friends had become bound together in an unholy alliance by drugs, Heavy Metal music and Satan worship. After the killing frenzy in which the victim was battered more than seventy times with a baseball bat, Hardy muttered, "Sacrifice to Satan" and dumped the body into a cistern he jokingly called "The Well of Hell." Of the Satan worship Hardy later said, "You can't just dabble in it. It sucks you in real quick . . . there was something definitely inside me."[10]

What most people do not realize is that occultic or satanic crime is fundamentally anti-Christian and that ultimately it results in contempt for or attacks on Christian beliefs, institutions, symbols and persons. When a Rhode Island governmental agency recently granted a tax exemption to a coven of witches, it was duped. Tax administrator R. Gary Clark issued his ruling on the basis that the coven met the guidelines for a church under a 1986 Rhode Island Supreme Court ruling. The agency accepted the evidence from the witches that they did not use their occultic powers for "destructive purposes."[11]

A prime symbol of the occult, in addition to the symbols for Satan and his underworld, is the *inverted cross.* Research any of the occult lore and the prominence of the inverted cross and ideas and practices which violate the teachings and symbols of Christ are legion. Some occult practices require the violation of a church or church altar for their practice.

Here is my point: This incredible explosion of involvement in the occult and satanic beliefs and practices is the bellwether of the coming persecution of Christians.

When the cross is turned upside down, it isn't long before Christians are turned upside down. And there is no question that Jesus Christ Himself predicted the persecution of His followers in the end time.

The stage is now set for increasing persecution of Christian believers.

10

Into the Black Hole

"They will lay hands on you and persecute you. They will deliver you to synagogues and prisons, and you will be brought before kings and governors, and all on account of my name . . . You will be betrayed by parents, brothers, relatives and friends, and they will put some of you to death. All men will hate you because of me."

Jesus Christ
Luke 21:12-17

☐   ☐   ☐

I believe strong evidence exists that worldwide persecution has begun on those who have a personal relationship with Jesus Christ. Christians are the most widely hated and persecuted group of people on earth today. Marxists persecute Christians from the Siberian labor camps to the Cuban prisons, from the Red Chinese communes to the midnight disappearances in Ethiopia and Mozambique. Muslims persecute Christians from the hostage cells of

Lebanon to the terrorist attacks in Morocco, Libya, Algeria and the Sudan. Animists persecute Christians at the instigation of their occult witch doctors in many parts of Africa and Asia.

According to the *World Christian Encyclopedia,* Christians in *two-thirds* of the nations of the world are experiencing some form of "religio-political restrictions," ranging from limitations on political freedoms and civil rights to outright attempts to suppress or eradicate their faith. Some 30 percent have no political freedom or adequate civil liberties.[1] Approximately one-fourth live under anti-Christian regimes while 13 percent live under atheistic ones. Nearly 17 percent are "experiencing severe state interference in religion, obstruction or harassment."[2]

Persecution in the U.S.A.

In the U. S. the most vicious attacks on Christians come from the gay and lesbian communities, the pro-abortion community, the national women's movement, the radical civil libertarians, the pornography industry, the television and film industries, and the political far left.

The homosexual community viciously harassed and badgered singer Anita Bryant and her husband a number of years ago after Ms. Bryant took a public stand against a Dade County, Florida, proposal that would give special legal status to homosexuals. Followed from city to city by gays, Anita and her manager/husband Bob Green received repeated death warnings, had concert after concert broken up by bomb threats and were locked out of contracts to perform. I attended one concert which was menaced by a bomb threat, picketed by gays and interrupted by a drug-using protester wearing a shirt linking Anita Bryant to fascism.

Deep into the torture of vilification by the press, cancelled performing engagements, and 'round the clock harassment, Bob Green tearfully told me, "Larry, we never asked for this." That torturous experience was a factor in the demise of Anita's career and their previously strong marriage.

In like manner, gay publications commonly carry vicious attacks on Christian ministers and governmental and civic leaders who oppose "gay rights."

Moguls of the pornography industry filed a harassment suit against members of Ronald Reagan's President's Commission on Pornography, demanding incredible financial damages. The helpless members of this official governmental commission, who were serving their country and their President at great personal cost and without pay, had all of their personal assets threatened. Dr. James Dobson, founder and president of Focus on the Family and a member of the President's Commission, told me of the debilitating impact that suit was having on him, his family and his ministry.

Porn publications, even the "less hard-core" magazines available in most convenience stores, are now the nation's leading forum for anti-Christian propaganda. They take great delight in ridiculing and damning the "religious right wing" and in lumping all Christians together as "fun-hating fundamentalists." Several of these periodicals have poured out whole series of scurrilous attacks against Donald Wildmon of the American Family Association, Jerry Falwell of what used to be the Moral Majority and other champions of morality and purity in media.

But mainstream film and TV producers are becoming decidedly anti-Christian as well. No sooner had the processing fluids dried on the film *The Last Temptation of Christ* than Universal Pictures was presented with a movie script in which evangelical Christians were the villains. No word has come out of the studio as to whether they intend to produce it, but even if they do not I believe another studio will.

Cinecom released a movie in late 1989 called *The Handmaid's Tale*. The *Los Angeles Times* described this as a "visionary tale in which religious fundamentalists have overthrown the government and the remaining fertile women are required to be their [personal] handmaids."[3] Lest you think that films like this are el cheapo productions, this one starred Robert Duvall, Faye Dunaway and Natasha Richardson, all performing heavyweights. These movies basically do one thing: They make it socially acceptable to demean and hate Christians.

The American Civil Liberties Union pursues an unceasing bitter campaign of legal harassment against Christians, Christian symbols and Christian practices, and Judeo-Christian values. In an incredible twisting of the principles of freedom of speech, freedom of religion and separation of church and state, this organization pursues efforts to legalize all forms of pornography (including child porn), legalize and legitimize all kinds of deviant sexual behavior as "victimless crimes" and expunge all vestiges of religious faith from public life. Not satisfied with the anti-faith nature of its opposition to including the words "under God" in the pledge of allegiance, in mid-1988 the ACLU sent a letter to the California Assembly Education Committee opposing a proposed sex education bill. The letter stated:

> It is our position that teaching that monogamous, heterosexual intercourse within marriage as a traditional American value is *an unconstitutional establishment of a religious doctrine in public schools.* There are various religions which hold contrary beliefs with respect to marriage and monogamy [emphasis added].[4]

Churches, Christian schools and other Christian structures have been the target of lawsuits by the ACLU all over America. Having debated ACLU representatives and lawyers on national radio and on television, I can say that those I debated were viciously anti-Christian.

Of even more concern is that such pointed, anti-Christian litigation is now being proposed by none other than the American Bar Association itself. In a seminar held in San Francisco in May of 1989, and sponsored by the Division for Professional Education of the ABA, attorneys were trained in the "expanding use of tort law against religions" and "tort law as an ideological weapon." The event brochure promoted the seminar for "attorneys who want to be on the leading edge of an explosive new area of law."[5] This use of tort law against religious organizations was described by several of the seminar speakers as "a nuclear weapon." The selling point of the seminar was that attorneys could make money using this ideological weapon against churches and religious organizations. Clearly, war has been declared and Christianity is in a fight to the death.

I know that Christians have opposition, but you're talking words, you may say. *When anti-Christian sentiment turns to physical violence, then maybe we will have something to worry about.*

Something to Worry About

This is a test. I will describe for you two true incidents. Your challenge is to determine the time and geographical setting of each. Simple, huh?

Incident 1

The police troops arrived in two vans late in the afternoon. Their orders were to locate any . . . sympathizers . . . . The police hauled hundreds of suspects into Market Square where the scene turned violent. Before arresting anyone, the authorities forced men and women to run a gauntlet of jeering, kicking, spitting troopers.

Their thirst for pain seemingly could not be quenched. They turned on women and children. A frail woman of sixty-six hid her sons from the attackers, and the police set upon her. "Where are your sons?" they demanded. Grabbing her by the hair, they dragged the sickly woman down the street. They hoped to wrench a confession either through her torment or humiliation before watching neighbors. But many neighbors, fearing for themselves, turned away. The woman was pulled to Market Square, her face bloodied as it scraped along the street. In the end her noble effort to spare her boys seemed foolish, as they were found and herded into the town square.[6]

Incident 2

The police . . . brought in a double-decker bus, complete with tinted windows (thus it was impossible to see what was going on inside the bus . . .). Brutality started on the bus. Angela was dragged onto the bus by her hair. People were billy-clubbed, kicked and punched. Police dragged women in the bus by pulling up skirts and bras over their heads, exposing them in so doing . . . . The men were denied food for thirty hours . . . . Upon arrival at the . . . jail there were over thirty police . . . lined up along five or six flights of stairs . . . . Women were then dragged up the steps, some by the hair and others by the neck. You could hear the sound of heads smacking against the steps. The warden was at the bottom of the first flight of stairs, and he kicked [the people] as they were dragged by him.

During this entire procedure there was foul language, obscenities, and threats of putting women . . . in rooms with male prisoners to be sodomized and raped . . . . They were asked to strip in front of male guards and male prisoners. All refused. They were then forcibly stripped by both male and female guards, dragged, kicked and punched. Women . . . were fondled, verbally abused and threatened.[7]

Give up?

Incident 1 is the description of troopers brutalizing Jews in a community in *World War II Nazi Germany.*

Incident 2 is the description of the police brutalizing Christians who were passively protesting outside an abortion clinic in *Pittsburgh, Pennsylvania, on March 11, 1989.*

The Screws Are Tightening

The mood is getting increasingly ugly for Christians. Soon, I predict, overt persecution of believers will be commonplace. Our kids will be beat up and sexually molested at school, forced to perform perverse acts by the youthful agents of the dark side. Our churches will be desecrated and worship services disrupted. Our homes will be vandalized and our lives threatened. Our cars will be damaged and our tires slashed.

Discrimination now in operation will become common and rampant. Ask Ted Baehr, founder and president of *Movieguide,* a biblical guide to movies and entertainment, about religious discrimination. One of his staff routinely called Paramount Pictures in Hollywood for movie stills of the film *Tucker* for their publication. *Movieguide* had chosen *Tucker* one of the best family films of the year. The head of the studio's licensing department told *Movieguide's* staff person they would not sell promotional stills to "fundamentalist Christians."[8] KFI Talk Radio, one of the oldest and biggest Los Angeles radio stations, recently had two call-in talk shows on the subject, "Is Christianity more trouble than it is worth?" Imagine the station doing that with Jews, Muslims, Hindus or atheists.

In a practice not that uncommon now, more and more Christian university professors will be denied tenure. Graduate students will be denied fellowships and even degrees for taking public stands for Christian values or holding biblical views on anything from sexual morality to marriage and family, from the origins of the earth and man to catastrophism. It will be more and more difficult to get high-ranking positions in major companies as a professing Christian.

Laws meant to punish evildoers will be twisted in their interpretations to prosecute Christians. As you read this, believers are being assessed treble court damages and are in threat of having all their assets seized as pro-abortion lawyers twist RICO *anti-racketeering laws* against pro-life demonstrators. The U. S. Court of Appeals for the Third Circuit ruled that entering health clinics to stop women from having abortions is a "racketeering activity."[9]

Jail sentences and fines for civil disobedience or other offenses will be disproportionately heavy for believers. A District Judge in Los Angeles levied a fine of $110,000, to be paid to the ACLU, on Operation Rescue for refusing to obey a court order to stop abortion rescues.[10] Randall Terry, leader of Operation Rescue, was given a two-year prison sentence for passive civil disobedience at an abortion clinic. And while I did not sympathize with evangelist Jim Bakker's financial misdeeds, it's interesting that he received a forty-five-year sentence with no parole for ten years—while convicted drug dealers serve an average of only 15.5 months in jail, according to federal drug czar William Bennett.

I predict an increase of Christians who become "missing persons" never to be seen again, some sacrificed in satanic rites as the young college student was sacrificed south of the U. S./Mexican border not long ago.

I believe the evidence is overwhelming that the collective, international degeneracy of the character of man described in the four previous chapters will be focused on the followers of the man from Nazareth. Out of the *fearstorm* will come occult forces which will turn society into a moral and spiritual black hole on the star-studded background of the heavens. Lucifer's Half-Century Plan, or its equivalent, will be in full operation, and the deceiving spirits will smell victory.

Earnest, right-living disciples of Jesus Christ will be sucked into this black hole of contempt, rejection, discrimination and persecution. But for the sustaining, supernatural power of their God, Christians will be in constant terror for their jobs, their property, their children and their lives . . .

. . . temporarily

Swept into the planetless, starless darkness of spiritual space by occult forces beyond their control, believers in the Messiah will cry out to their God, their king, their Savior, their deliverer. The whole world will watch to see if He exists, if He rules, if He hears, if He delivers.

Take a deep breath. This dark passage—for it is only a passage and not a destination—through the black hole is foretold by the prophetic seers of the Bible.

The vision continues to unfold.

11

Don't Worry, Be Happy!

"Then the King will say to those on His right, 'Come, you who are blessed by my Father; take your inheritance, the kingdom prepared for you since the creation of the world . . . '

"Then He will say to those on His left, 'Depart from me, you who are cursed, into the eternal fire prepared for the Devil and his angels . . . ' "

Jesus Christ
Matthew 25:34,41

☐   ☐   ☐

The Bible generally gets a bum rap. Intellectuals give it a hard time, alleging that it is filled with inconsistencies, mistakes and irrelevancies. Cultists pick and choose verses from it to stick into their false systems to give them an aura of religious respectability. Cynics proclaim, even in show tunes, "The things that you're liable to read in the

Bible ain't necessarily so."

Scientists don't like it because it conflicts with their pet theories—even though the Bible, rightly interpreted, has a better record of scientific consistency than the theories of the scientists. Jews like parts of the Bible but not the part that declares Jesus to be their Messiah. The immoral despise the Bible for being too narrow and puritanical.

A handful profess to believe the Bible, but find it more useful for a coffee table decoration than a perfect guide for faith and conduct. The masses don't like it but haven't read enough of it to tell you why they don't like it. A lot of theologians read it but have such a jolly time trying to get it to fit into some harebrained human philosophy or intellectual hypothesis that they miss the Person and spiritual benefit of the book. Literature profs give you a lot of palaver about the literary beauty of biblical writings but can't find Ezekiel. If they do, they don't have the foggiest notion what his prophecies mean.

Many come up with high-sounding quotations which they impute to the Bible. Then they are steamed when you tell them that "God helps those who help themselves" isn't in there. Most know just enough about the Bible to be dangerous, like the little girl who was asked what the Bible had to say about lying. Her answer: "A lie is an abomination unto the Lord and an ever present help in time of trouble."

A lot of church people read the Bible to get ammunition for the petty doctrinal battles they are having with other churches and denominations. The hyper-zealous use verses from the Bible as blunt instruments to bludgeon others into their way of thinking.

But I think the biggest reason why the Bible gets a

bum rap is that it teaches precepts that are so other-world-ly that they are totally ludicrous to the unaided human mind. Who doesn't struggle with the teaching to "love your enemies" when it's such great fun to hate them? Who doesn't balk at the notion of "turning the other cheek" when the pain from being struck is so excruciating? Who doesn't choke at the idea of "rejoicing in all things" when there is so much damnable agony on the planet? Who doesn't swallow hard on Jesus' "no man comes to the Father except through me" when that would rule out so many earnest and sincere friends of other faiths? Who doesn't struggle with the apparent absurdity of the Bible's formula for gaining wealth: Give as much as possible away, because "in whatever measure you give, it will be given to you, pressed down, shaken together, and running over"?

The Bible is *impossible!*

One Bible teacher, so struck by the "impossibility" of the Bible, declared, "Whenever I approach a situation, I think, 'Now what would be my normal, natural response?' Then I ask, 'Now what would be the *exact opposite* of my natural response?' " He says he finds that the Bible more often teaches the opposite response.

I'll have to admit, I've been setting you up.

You have slogged with me through ten chapters of some of the most miserable, frightening, disturbing stuff imaginable. By now I have laid on you a mix of biblical prophecy and real life data so stunning that it probably has you reeling. Yet, here you are with me in Chapter 11. *You're terrific!* There were times when I thought I was going to lose you.

Now I am going to share what the Bible says should be our response to all of this present and impending doom. Ready?

"Be Happy!"

Gimme a break, Poland! I've got my world coming apart at the seams, the underworld unleashing a satanic attack on me, my house being shaken to bits by earthquakes, a new world economic system shutting down my ability to buy bread, my neighbors persecuting my socks off, and you're trying to tell me the Bible wants me to be happy? *Get serious.*

I'm as serious as a funeral. That's what the Bible teaches *if* you are in the right category.

Whaddaya mean, "right category"?

You know the old saying about "separating the sheep from the goats"? You may not have known that that expression is from a Bible passage relating to the end times.

Here's the story. Much of the prophetic content that was uttered by Jesus and referred to in the first ten chapters of this book comes from a long talk He gave sitting on the Mount of Olives. That talk was recorded in Matthew 24. Jesus' talk continues into Chapter 25 with this sheep/goat story, edited for brevity:

> When the Son of Man comes in His glory, and all the angels with Him, He will sit on His throne in heavenly glory. All the nations will be gathered before Him, and He will separate the people one from another as a shepherd *separates the sheep from the goats.* He will put the *sheep* on His right and the *goats* on His left.
>
> Then the King will say to those on His right, "Come, you who are blessed by my Father; take your inheritance, the kingdom prepared for you since the creation of the world . . . ."
>
> Then He will say to those on His left, "Depart from me, you who are cursed, into the eternal fire prepared for the Devil and his angels . . . ."

Then they will go away to eternal punishment, but
the righteous to eternal life [emphasis added].[1]

See what I mean about the right category? The
category you are in makes all the difference in the world to
you during the last generation.

I don't think I need to draw a picture of what happens
to the goats. They'll be able to attend Lucifer's lectures at
the Demonic High Council Headquarters. The goats should
fit right in, what with their cloven hoofs and all.

Later I'll deal with the question of how people in the
goat category can get into the sheep category, but, for now,
I'm just going to talk to all the sheep readers.

Welcome, wooly friend.

God knows that the normal, natural response to all
this unleashing of heartache is to get frightened and discouraged. He also knows that fear and discouragement are
the language of hell, not heaven. They are goat responses.
So the first directive for preparing for the coming persecution is . . .

1. Don't Let Your Heart Get Down

Jesus plopped this exhortation right in the middle of
His talk on signs of the end of the age:

Be careful or your hearts will be weighed down with
dissipation, drunkenness, and the anxieties of life, and
that day will close on you unexpectedly like a trap. For it
will come upon all those who live on the face of the whole
earth.[2]

God recognizes that things will be so tough that even
the *sheep* will be tempted to be discouraged or escape into
heavy drinking or let the anxieties of life get to them. Jesus

exhorts them not to let that happen.

The only way I've found to carry out this directive is to draw a line down the middle of the page representing my life. On one side of the page I write, "God's Responsibility." On the other side I write, "My Responsibility." Since Jesus promised that His yoke is "easy" and His burden is "light,"[3] I figure I must have dragged a God-sized responsibility onto my side of the page when life is "hard" and "heavy."

You know what? I have found that nearly everything on my side of the page can be subsumed under one of three categories: love, trust, obey. If I can just keep doing these three, life is bearable—even enjoyable.

2. Watch and Pray

The second word of counsel from Jesus is:

> Be always on the watch, and pray that you may be able to escape all that is about to happen, and that you may be able to stand before the Son of Man.[4]

I've never been one of those masochistic pray-ers who cry, "O Lord, bruise me, bake me, break me! Whatever you have to do to make me!" I'm too chicken. Instead I pray, "O Lord, give me such a teachable spirit and submissive will that You won't have to break me to get me to shape up." You can count on me to pray for an escape route; I have His permission.

Then, too, the "watch and pray" formula is a perfect balance. It's really hard to be praying if you haven't been watching. How do you know what to pray about or pray for?

Also, if we aren't watching, we'll be so out of it on what's happening that the coming of Christ will catch us "like a trap" when we least expect it. That's like dropping a dollar bill at a baseball game and bending over to pick it up only to miss seeing a home run, the only run in the three-hour game.

It's equally nonsensical to be watching if you aren't praying. A keen observer of what is happening is going to be under the pile in no time. He'll have all that hideous data and nothing constructive to do with it. That's why we ought to pray through the six o'clock news. We don't need all of that information about the ruin in the world if we're not going to take it to God in prayer. If you're watching without praying, forget the news. You'll be happier not knowing it. You need to pray to be able to *cope* with what you observe.

With all the deceptive signals abroad in the world, prayer is also indispensable for *interpreting* what you observe. For instance, Paul said that the worst of the persecution would break into world affairs "like a thief in the night. While people are saying, 'Peace and safety,' destruction will come on them suddenly . . . and they will not escape."[5]

How do we respond, then, when the Soviet Union pulls out of Afghanistan and acknowledges that its Afghan foray was ill-conceived? What does it mean when Russia begins to disarm unilaterally in some areas, remove its military presence from other strategic locations in the world and proclaim *glastnost* and *perestroika*? How do we interpret a democratic government in Poland, radical reforms in Hungary and other Warsaw Pact nations, and the East German government's breaking down of the Berlin wall, creating a "peace and safety" euphoria for millions? Do we head for the beach or the bomb shelters? Only prayer will enable us to decide.

The wrap-up on this advice is to pray "that you may be able to stand before the Son of Man." If you've been keeping your heart up and your head clear, and have been praying for an escape route and a way to stand in His presence, you'll get your requests. You're just the kind of person He's looking for.

3. Don't Be Alarmed During the "Birth Pains"

Remember the "Labor Pains" chapter? There we talked about the *beginnings* of the birth pains.

1. A significant and widespread increase in famines.

2. A significant and widespread increase in earthquakes.

3. A dramatic increase in the number of phony "messiahs."

4. A radical increase in national and ethnic wars and war rumors.

5. A predominance of intellectual and religious scoffers who ridicule the notion of the waning era of man or of any impending catastrophe.

6. A radical degeneration in the collective character of man.

According to Matthew's account, Jesus directs us not to sweat it during the *beginnings* of the birth pains:

> . . . but see to it that you are not alarmed. Such things must happen, but the end is still to come.[6]

I personally believe that this list of "labor pains" pinpoints our generation on God's timetable, and we are just about to turn the corner in human history from the *beginnings* to the *followings* of the birth pains. For now, though, don't let fear get you. Even when things do get worse, we must remember that "God did not give us [the sheep] a spirit of timidity, but a spirit of power, of love, and of self-discipline."[7]

4. Don't Go Chasing After False "Messiahs"

As Matthew continues his account of this same talk, he quotes Jesus as saying:

> At that time if anyone says to you, "Look, here is the Christ!" or "There he is!" do not believe it. For false Christs and false prophets will appear and perform great signs and miracles to deceive even the elect – if that were possible. See, I have told you ahead of time.
>
> So if anyone tells you, "There he is, out in the desert," do not go out; or "Here he is, in the inner rooms," do not believe it. For as the lightning comes from the east and flashes to the west, so will be the coming of the Son of Man. Wherever there is a carcass, there the vultures will gather.[8]

The religious snake oil salesmen have always been around. But there is always a greater demand for religious quacks when things are tough all over. We have more than our share today. As the persecution increases and the out-pouring of the wrath of God begins on the world, there will be a bumper crop of "fox hole believers," those who suddenly get really "spiritual" as the shells explode around them. They'll begin looking for spiritual deliverers. Preying on the fearstorm and the increasing hostility of the global environment, messiah pushers will show up everywhere.

They'll be impressive too. These messiahs will be able to do miracles – *real* miracles. Jesus says, "*Great* signs and miracles." Your mother-in-law may be swept into this because she is healed of her arthritis. Your son may join a false messiah's cult after seeing an amputee's limb grow back before his eyes or hearing audible voices from the heavens. Miracles are not proof of divine origin. Satan works miracles too. Remember that the magicians of Moses' day duplicated 80 percent or more of the miracles God wrought on Pharaoh.

Jesus' advice? Don't even waste your time seeking out one of their meetings. And take special notice of how Jesus closes His case on this point: "Wherever there is a carcass, there the vultures will gather." As the decaying corpse of human civilization rots away from its own self-delusions, degenerative spiritual diseases and character disorders, there will be plenty of vultures there to benefit from the situation.

These vultures are the smooth-talking kind, like *The Music Man's* Professor Harold Hill. The apostle Paul describes them as the people "who worm their way into homes and gain control over weak-willed women, who are loaded down with sins and are swayed by all kinds of evil desires, always learning but never able to acknowledge the truth."[9]

Don't be swept in by them!

But how, you may say, *will we know the true Christ when He returns?*

This prophecy makes it extremely clear that it will be made extremely clear. The coming of the true deliverer will be as clear and visible as lightning in the eastern sky to people in the west.

5. Keep Your Lifestyle Lean and Clean

Jesus declared that when the worst of the persecution comes, prudent people will flee to safety without going back for any of their *stuff.* He states it this way:

> Let no one on the roof of his house go down to take
> anything out of the house. Let no one in the field go back
> to get his cloak.[10]

The admonition had to be given with American sheep
in mind. When comedian George Carlin discusses the *stuff*
we Americans have accumulated, he suggests that one
thing that makes travel so uncomfortable for us is that,
however briefly, we are separated from our stuff. We try to
compensate for the uncomfortability by carrying suitcases,
boxes, garment bags and foot lockers of our stuff with us
on the trip.

When we arrive at our destinations, we immediately
worry about whether our stuff is going to arrive safely. If
it does, we instantly start taking out our stuff and arrang-
ing it. But we are never really comfortable traveling, Carlin feels, because wherever we are, we are among *other
people's stuff* and separated from our own. One of the joys
of getting home is being back with our own stuff.

The one who survives the persecution won't dare be
attached to his stuff. Thievery will be so common that he'll
have a lot of his stuff stolen. Vandalism will be such an
everyday occurrence that he'll have a lot of his stuff
damaged or destroyed. Earthquakes will be so frequent and
destructive that he'll have lots of stuff shaken to rubble.

If he has any sense, when it is time to flee to safety, he
won't even look back at his stuff. The end times will be so
chaotic that attachment to material things may keep a person from surviving. Remember, anything you can't aban-
don in the interests of survival you don't own; *it owns you.*
Live lean and clean materially—as if your stuff doesn't
amount to anything—because it doesn't.

6. Do Faithfully What You're Supposed to Be Doing

Again, in the long talk Jesus gave on last days matters, He shared excellent advice for those living in the terminal era: *Make sure you're doing what God wants you to be doing.* Jesus illustrated this advice with an example of a servant whose master put him in charge of food service for the household servants while he went away:

> It will be good for that servant whose master finds him doing so [caring for the servants' provision as instructed] when he returns. I tell you the truth, he will put him in charge of all his possessions. But suppose that servant is wicked and says to himself, "My master is staying away a long time," and he begins to beat his fellow servants and to eat and drink with the drunkards. The master of that servant will come on a day when he does not expect him and at an hour he is not aware of. He will cut him to pieces and assign him a place with the hypocrites, where there will be weeping and gnashing of teeth.[11]

Rare is the man or woman who, in the tiny voice in the inner person, has not heard, "This isn't something you should be doing with your life" or "I want you to do this with your life." Jesus' counsel in Matthew is two dimensional. It deals with *what* every person is to be doing and *how* he is to be doing it.

The what: The steward in this example was supposed to be caring for the provisions for the other servants. Vocationally his assignment was clear, and the steward who pursued his master-given calling was given a much more significant position upon the master's return. The steward who "turned wicked" got so preoccupied during the long absence of his master with his own eating, drinking and carousing that he pursued an agenda of his own making. That spelled trouble.

The how: The steward was to discharge his master-assigned duties with precise obedience and the utmost dependability. The one who turned wicked became careless because of his master's long absence. He abused his authority and responsibility, took matters into his own hands and pursued his own pleasures rather than the given tasks.

The moral: The Master is going to take excellent care of the person who, despite the difficulty of the coming persecution and the long-term absence of his Master, sticks faithfully to what his Master has called him to do. He'll get a significant promotion and perks. If God has directed you to serve Him by being the best educator in the country, don't sell storm windows. If God has called you to serve Him in ministry, don't you dare be an educator.

Whatever the Master calls you to do, don't get careless during His delayed return. If you take this counsel seriously, you may have to change jobs or be a whole lot more conscientious about the one you have.

7. Stand for Right and Don't Sweat Your Defense

When things keep coming at you, it is natural to figure you must be in the wrong lane, and that the reasonable thing to do is change into another. This won't be a reasonable conclusion during the time of persecution, because things will be coming at *everybody*. Changing lanes may be the worst thing you could do.

One of the visual images I have from childhood comic books is that of Superman flying in over a railroad track and straight-arming a freight train to a halt. That was sheer inspiration for a kid who had visions of taking on the world and winning. It's also not a bad image for the believer in the time of persecution.

The Commander directs His troops to stand up and be counted at the outset of the persecution epoch:

> When these things [the horrific birth pains] begin to take place, stand up and lift up your heads, because your redemption is drawing near.[12]

In another place in the talk He exhorts:

> He who stands firm to the end will be saved.[13]

The whole concept of taking a stand for righteousness is woven throughout biblical literature and is given a strong presentation in the "armor of God" instruction in the writings of the apostle Paul:

> Therefore, put on the full armor of God so that *when the day of evil comes,* you may be able to stand your ground, and after you have done everything, to stand. Stand firm then . . . [emphasis added].[14]

There's a great progression in these three passages. The first one says: *Get up and look up.* The second one instructs: *Take a position and hold the position to the end.* The third one commands: *Make an aggressive, military stand against what the enemy is doing and put everything you have into it.* In essence, supernaturally empowered believers are to fly into the path of the oncoming freight train and raise the hand of resistance. Nobody else on earth is going to.

So much for shrinking-violet Christians. So much for wimpianity. So much for a society in which more than 80 million people who claim to be "born again" don't have enough gumption to stand against the flood of evil that is washing over their land.

But, yikes, Larry! you may be thinking. *If there is this*

hideous, occult outpouring against us Christians, how will
we defend ourselves?

Jesus Christ thought of everything. In this same in-
formation-packed presentation, He acknowledged that the
persecutors will "lay hands on you and persecute you . . .
deliver you to synagogues and prisons, and you will be
brought before kings and governors, and all on account of
my name."[15]

Your response? Here's what to do:

But *make up your mind not to worry* beforehand
how you will defend yourselves. For I will give you words
and wisdom that *none of your adversaries will be able to
resist or contradict* [emphasis added].[16]

In college men's glee club we sang:

Give me some men who are stouthearted men who
will fight for the right they adore.
Start me with ten who are stouthearted men, and
I'll soon give you 10,000 more!

That's the appropriate response. Much of the Church
has been singing:

Give us an out 'cause we don't have the clout to
engage in a war for the right.
Head out the back with our straggly pack, and we
all can be gone overnight!

A Christian who won't stand for something will fall
for anything.

8. Make Your Spiritual Life Your Top Priority

Isn't it about time we got our priorities turned

rightside up? It seems that most American "sheep" give precious little thought to the desires of the Shepherd. The priority list for the average American goes something like this: money, work, pleasure, family and God — in that order. Even if these aren't your priorities, God ends up near the bottom of most lists.

We can no longer afford to live by this upside-down agenda. This is made unmistakably clear in these prophetic words from Peter:

> The heavens will disappear with a roar; the elements will be destroyed by fire, and the earth and everything in it will be laid bare. Since everything will be destroyed in this way, what kind of people ought you to be? You ought to live holy and godly lives as you look forward to the day of God and speed its coming.[17]

And from Jude:

> In the last times there will be scoffers . . . . But you, dear friends, build yourselves up in your most holy faith and pray in the Holy Spirit. Keep yourselves in God's love as you wait for the mercy of our Lord Jesus Christ to bring you to eternal life.[18]

Not a bad formula for spiritual health: building your faith, praying in the Spirit, abiding in God's love, waiting for God's mercy, living holy and godly lives.

If your faith is weak, you'll never believe God through the persecution. If you aren't praying in the Spirit, which means being controlled by the Spirit as you pray, your prayer life will be impotent at a time when you need it to be mighty. If you're not abiding in God's love, you're going to be overcome with hatred at the hideous evil that is being done to you and others. If you don't wait for God's mercy to be demonstrated, you will collapse from the pressure of

His wrath. If you don't live a holy and godly life, you'll be swept into the maelstrom of evil with the rest of the planet.

So much for me, but I have kids. I shudder to think what they are going to face in this terrifying time of world persecution. What should I do about them?

9. Get Your Parenting Act Together

I have six kids. Pick an age, any age. I have sons and daughters. I have one in law school, one in a design university, one in a liberal arts college, one in high school and two in elementary school. The oldest is twenty-two and the youngest is six. My wife and I figured out that we will be eligible for senior citizen passes to our youngest's high school games.

I tell you this to establish some credibility. I'm sure you've heard of the lady who had six theories on child rearing and no children. Later she had six children and no theories! My wife and I have six children and three principles that have carried us successfully through an aggregate *ninety-two years* of parenting. I fully expect that these principles will carry us through the time of persecution as well.

The Big Three: (1) Make parenting a top priority; (2) get your own act together; and (3) teach your act to your kids.

Make parenting a top priority. We tend to do better at the things we make a priority. It is no mystery to me why most Americans fail at parenting. They don't make successful parenting a top priority. Being an outstanding parent is number three on my list of goals after being an outstanding Christian and an outstanding husband. My wife and I are surely a long way from being perfect parents, but we're up there with the best of them as judged by our community *and* our kids. Make parenting number 32 on your priority list and you'll be a 32nd rate parent. There isn't a lot of mystery about that.

Get your own act together. Modeling is the single most powerful dimension of parenting. Frighteningly, our kids become what we *are* more than what we *proclaim.* You know very well that you are more like your parents than you care to admit.

The implications of this are terrorizing. If you don't make your kids a priority by giving them your time and attention, they will decide they aren't very important. If you cut out on your spouse, your kids will determine that marital fidelity isn't required. If you divorce, they will determine that marriage vows are dispensable. If you show contempt for them, they will determine that they are contemptible. If you sacrifice them for achievements, they will decide that achievements are more important than people. If money is more important to you than your integrity, they will sell their souls to get money. If you participate in filthy entertainment, they will find filth entertaining. If you shred them or others with your tongue, *amazingly* they will become smart-mouthed and sarcastic.

If you never read the Bible, they will determine that the Bible is an irrelevant book. If you never pray, they will view prayer as a waste of time. If involvement in church is slightly below going to the beach in priority, they'll live their lives spending Sundays with beach people instead of with God's people.

Evil kids are a whole lot rarer in homes with righteous parents. The sins of the fathers which are visited on third and fourth generations are more often than not "visited" by parental modeling.

Teach your act to your kids. My wife and I are greatly

annoyed at a comment we get occasionally from parents struggling with problems with their offspring. They'll say, "Yeah, but you've got *great* kids!" We resent that remark. We didn't just happen to get kids from a *good* batch while other parents got theirs from a *bad* batch. *All children come from a bad batch.* They all arrive in this world with a sin nature, with a rebellious streak and with disgusting arrogance. They all come sickeningly selfish, too. Kids have to be *taught,* and most teaching comes with firm, loving discipline.

Proverbs says, "A kid's heart is filled with rebellion, and the only way to drive it out of him is through discipline."[19] It isn't enough for the parents to have *their* acts together. They have to team up to administer instruction and loving discipline until the kid gets *his* act together. Once he does, he'll weather any storm, even the storm of global persecution.

10. Be Happy

I know I said this before, but the Bible, that *impossible* book, also declares it more than once — even in the face of devastating world oppression. Jesus' words to His disciples appear either supernatural or stupid:

> Blessed are you when men hate you, when they exclude you and insult you and reject your name as evil because of the Son of Man. Rejoice in that day and leap for joy, because great is your reward in Heaven. For that is how their fathers treated the prophets.[20]

This command is even more than "be happy." This is *rejoice, leap for joy* and take the persecution as a *blessing.*

Is that ridiculous or what? No, it is not. Two notations in the command explain why it's supernatural and not stupid. First, you are not the first to suffer for your faith. Others have suffered, and it all worked out for them. Secondly, "great is your reward in heaven." There is extravagant payoff for anything you suffer. Jesus promised it in another of His declarations.

One day Peter, quick-tongued as he was, said, "Lord, we have left everything to follow you. What's in it for us?"

Can you believe that question? Well, I think if we're honest we've all had that question at one time or another. Listen to Jesus' response:

> Everyone who has left houses or brothers or sisters or father or mother or children or fields for my sake will receive *a hundred times as much and will inherit eternal life* [emphasis added].[21]

No wonder we are to rejoice, whistle, shout, clap, cheer, dance and leap for joy when we are persecuted. The deal is that for every loss you suffer, you get repaid *one hundred times the amount* and receive *eternal life for a bonus*. If I told you of an investment where you could get one hundred times what you put in with eternal life as a bonus, would you be interested?

The more evil our enemies do to us, the more our reward goes up—by a ratio of 100 to 1. That's why Jesus called persecution a blessing. So the *worse* things get for the sheep, the *better* things actually get for the sheep . . . and the *worse* things get for the goats.

Hey, sheep! Don't worry! Be happy!

Sometime in the future.
By one who remained faithful.

12

Glory, Glory, Hallelujah!

"Now the dwelling of God is with men, and he will live with them. They will be his people, and God himself will be with them and be their God. He will wipe every tear from their eyes. There will be no more death or mourning or crying or pain, for the old order of things has passed away."

Jesus Christ
Revelation 21:3,4

☐   ☐   ☐

How time flies. It's been more than nine hundred years since the day of deliverance. And what a day that was. Life has been so overwhelmingly wonderful during these nine centuries that I haven't even thought of time. But, then, I guess time isn't that important when you have an unlimited supply of it.

If it weren't for the mind expansion we all received

with our new bodies, it would probably be hard to remember back to my Earth hour. There I used to struggle with what heaven would be like. When I was a kid, I had a lot of questions about what would happen after I died. I wondered if I could take my Swiss army knife with me or if heaven had even better pocket knives.

I surely hoped God would let kids have electric trains and remote control boats. Sometimes I'd get real excited that maybe in heaven kids could fly their own jet planes and God would fix it so they would just automatically know how to fly them. If they hit the wrong button, He would make sure they wouldn't crash. I didn't figure it would be heaven if planes could crash. I had that pretty well figured out. What I didn't think of was that you might be able to go places in an instant like we can here — without flying.

I also remember worrying some about what we would do *forever*. I would get a sick feeling thinking that maybe we'd have to spend eternity in church. I figured that even if Jesus Himself preached and did miracles, it would eventually get pretty boring. Crazy notions, but I was just a kid, and that was 940 years ago. Now I *know*.

Once I got here it didn't take long to get over the heartaches of the Earth hour. Actually, compared to many of the people in Adam's race, I guess the first half of my life was pretty great. Until I was out of college I could still operate pretty freely as a believer. I didn't have any trouble buying things, and there were still pockets of other believers who, by being cautious, could pretty well escape the violence. Then things deteriorated rapidly.

For a scriptural basis for the fictional scenario presented in this chapter, see Appendix B, "Biblical Background for the Nature of Christ's Second Coming."

The Worsened World

Yet there was a bright spot in my life. I fell madly in love with Maria and married her right after college. Our first year of marriage went pretty well. Our relationship was wonderful, like one long honeymoon, but things were touch-and-go in our circumstances. My job at the University bookstore kept bread on the table and the excitement over Maria's pregnancy toward the end of that year gave us a lot of joy. But joy from life on earth got increasingly scarce.

The first devastating thing in our marriage was my getting fired from the bookstore. The manager said that the University wasn't employing Christians anymore. He said the board of regents had ruled that the Christian lifestyle and world view were "incompatible with a free academic environment" and that the employment of Christians was a "violation of the principle of separation of church and state for a public university." Obviously, I wasn't the only one to be let go. Those of us who were fired struggled with resentment against those we knew were believers but had lied about it to keep their jobs.

It was no secret that the University power structure at every level despised us believers. Among other things, they were contemptuous of our non-participation in the spring and fall orgies, which is what Homecoming and Springfest had become. Then, too, I almost didn't get my degree when the head of my department found out that I viewed homosexuality as a "perversion." He was livid. He recommended a denial of permission to graduate. If the bureaucracy hadn't held up his recommendation so that it didn't get considered before commencement, I probably wouldn't have gotten my degree.

No, I shouldn't say that. Maria and I and some other believing friends had prayed to the King. I found out since

I got here that it was He, not the bureaucracy, that got my degree through the system. Praise the King! I've been finding out a lot of things I couldn't have known during the Earth hour.

It was really hard getting jobs back then if you were a believer. Employers knew they were asking for harassment if they hired you. Strange and malicious things happened to establishments which did hire Christians—vandalism, sabotage to their communications and data processing systems, vendors who would suddenly refuse to do business with them, loss of customers. Some believers lied, denying they were followers of the way, to get jobs, but it often didn't work. So many people attended New Age worship centers and were so sensitized spiritually that they could tell you were a Christian by your aura, even if you weren't walking with the King.

Then there was the problem of The Mark. Near the turn of the century, an international, financial plan called Consolibank was launched and coordinated by the global banking community which the Japanese dominated. The plan seemed innocent enough and even smart at the time. It did away with all credit cards and coordinated all of the world's finances on a Galactichip system. Galactichips replaced the computer systems we had been using.

Cashed Out

With the new system nobody had cash. All credits and debits to personal and organizational accounts were done by Galactichip transfers. One of Consolibank's selling points to the world's nations was that Galactichip transfers would shut down the global drug trade by making cash transactions impossible. That worked until the world government legalized the drug trade for its own control and profit.

I'll admit the Galactichip system was a great idea. It was so much more efficient than anything we had ever had before. There was just the problem of The Mark. Everybody had to get a laser-imprinted mark on his forehead. It was really surgically imprinted, a kind of radioactive writing. It appeared as a fine scratch when first done, but in a few days was invisible except to the Markreader machines which nearly everybody had.

Believers (the courageous ones, that is) refused to take The Mark. The entire financial system was geared to Mark purchases, so even to buy a tube of toothpaste without The Mark caused the salesclerk to go through an incredible hassle. From the launching of the system believers were a thorn in the side of merchants. Eventually the world government got all member nations to outlaw non-Mark IDs. That made it impossible for Maria and me to buy anything. On top of that, we couldn't go through a toll road gate, couldn't park in a parking garage, couldn't get a driver's license, couldn't pay our taxes . . . The list was endless. We became hated outcasts of the system.

How many times I came home to find Maria sobbing on the sofa. She so wanted to be a good wife and mother, but she just couldn't. Everything she wanted to do to show her love for me required The Mark. The frustration was unbearable.

Sweet Charity

The arrival of precious little Charity was a source of great joy to us. We praised the King that her home birth was normal. Had there been complications, no hospital would have taken Maria without The Mark. With the world outside our doors growing more hostile to us on a daily basis, family became a key source of joy. When I was a kid and things were better in society, it seemed my mom and dad and my brother and I took family for granted. My parents didn't spend much time with us kids. It was very different for Maria and me. *Faith* and *family* made life bearable.

Church was another story. Most of the Christian church buildings had been converted into New Age worship centers. The churches had died spiritually around the turn of the century and the persecution had intimidated the rest into closing. Churches couldn't even accept or process contributions without The Mark. But the few identifiable believers left were a whole lot stronger in their faith. It seemed that the worse things got for us, the stronger our faith became.

Home meetings became our church services. We varied the times and the places and sometimes met in early morning hours so we could slip into services under cover of darkness. Neighbors got furious if they discovered us. It was against the zoning laws to have Christian meetings in residential areas.

When Charity reached school age, we had gotten pretty good at coping. The garden and the communal food sharing with other believers provided pretty well for us. The King was so faithful. When the fridge was empty, we'd pray and the garden would seemingly explode with produce or a sack of groceries would show up on our porch. We never knew where the groceries came from — most likely from a secret believer who had accepted The Mark and could buy.

Home school was the only alternative for Charity. Christian schools had been outlawed by the federal government as "subversive," and the state system was teaching New Age spiritualism to first graders. The afternoon nap was replaced by a meditation and mantra-chanting session. Sex education, in which kids from grade one through high school participated in classroom experimentation with various sex acts, was a required part of the curriculum. This was promoted as an attempt to educate the whole society to "sexual freedom and fulfillment." The objective was to make every child a bisexual by sixth grade, thus eliminating the "stigma" attached to homosexuality and lesbianism.

Psychic Phenomena classes were standard curricular offerings from junior high on. Essentially they were Satan worship sessions thinly disguised as "psychic science." A believer wouldn't have lasted a minute in one of those classes.

We had to exclude more and more of the media from our lives as we entered the turn of the century. Even children's cartoons had become sexually explicit and filled with satanic themes. Primetime TV was dominated by stories of sexual perversion, occultic horror, slasher movies and sadomasochistic practices. We would try to turn on the evening news to keep up with what was going on in the world, but even the news had sexually explicit "features." And the promos for other programs were so hideous that they made our effort futile.

Corner video stores had all become pornography stores. They just couldn't rent or sell "family" videos anymore. They were too tame and wouldn't provide the necessary profit margin. Going to the theater was unthinkable for believers, even if we could have gotten in without The Mark.

Heart Attack

Amazingly, the peace of Christ became more and more real to us as the hostility increased against us. We had bullets shot through our windows by rampaging gangs, but the police had a habit of looking the other way when the victims happened to be Christians. In truth, the police had become just another kind of criminal element protecting only their selected interests.

I hadn't owned a car for years. No Mark, no driver's license. Even the bicycle I rode was regularly stolen or vandalized. The believers had established an underground bicycle pool to keep the breadwinners in transportation. Most of us worked day labor and mostly for those whom we suspected were secret believers. They paid us in goods which we traded among each other for the things we needed.

Through all this hardship true believers had a spectacular, unexplainable peace. Our fellowship times were so precious to us. The embraces and holy kisses were deep expressions of affection. We seldom met that we didn't weep with joy over the blessings of the King and with heartache over the agony other members of the family of God were going through. One couple lost a daughter, kidnapped for a satanic sacrifice. They found her mutilated remains on their front lawn forty-two days after she had disappeared. The police did nothing.

Believe it or not, our little family actually remained happy through it all. Passages of Scripture about suffering and persecution became life blood to us spiritually. We saw the power of God heal our sicknesses when hospital care was out of the question for non-Mark people. We saw a steady flow of gays, Satan worshippers and masochists come to belief in the King. What a joy to watch the liberation that redemption brought them! One of the members of the coven who sacrificed our friends' daughter came to faith in Christ. She became a bold and powerful witness for Christ, even though witnessing (the state called it "proselyting" and an "attack on American pluralism") was now outlawed. Amazingly, we were all genuinely happy!

Joyful! Filled with praise and thankfulness to the King!

When God gave us little Daniel, we were overwhelmed with His goodness. Daniel was Daddy's joy. As he grew, our father-son "wrestling matches" on the family room floor, fishing trips, soccer on the front lawn, or picnics in the nearby parks bonded us into a loving unit. At age four, Daniel had trusted Jesus as Savior and had that marvelously simple faith in the King we seem to lose as we grow older. Danny and I often prayed and talked about "the King's business" together.

While I was at work one afternoon, Maria called on the Communiphone, hysterical. She screamed and sobbed out the words, "Come home, come home. It's Daniel."

Oh dear God, no! I thought as I ran to my bicycle and raced homeward. Breathlessly bursting across the lawn to the gate, I disarmed the security system to grant me entry.

Daniel lay in a pool of blood on the cement of the back patio. His face was cut, bruised and swollen nearly beyond recognition. Blood oozed out of his lower abdomen and below his belt line near his genitalia. Maria was leaning over him, sobbing. He was breathing but unconscious. I threw myself onto his body and screamed, "Oh God, Oh God, why Daniel? Why Daniel? Why not *me* instead of Daniel?" I sobbed out a prayer for healing. I begged God to protect me from the hatred and violence I felt welling up within me.

Danny was never the same. He lived, if you can call the quality of life he had after that "living."

We pieced the story together from bits and pieces of rumor and fact, mostly from kids and friends of kids of the believers in our area.

Daniel was on his way to a friend's house when a

teenage gang piled out of a car and kidnapped him. They were crazed with drugs, had Death Metal music blaring on the car CD player and had just come from some kind of occultic seance. They wanted Danny for sexual kicks. They thought it would be great sport to molest a Christian kid. When Danny refused to cooperate, the thugs became violent and started pummeling him around the face and head with their wrists, on which they wore leather straps with sharp metal studs.

For their final act of violence, the gang decided "If Mr. Jesus Freak doesn't want to have sex, we'll make sure he *never* does!" The brain damage and mutilation which followed left my precious little son mentally dull and maimed for the rest of his life.

Purgatory

I grew up Protestant, so I had never heard much about purgatory. Not finding the doctrine taught in the Bible, I never believed in it as something that anyone would experience after death. But I sure experienced it in life. The next four years until the deliverance were hideous. Every time I looked into the vapid eyes of my precious little Danny, I had to fight off bitterness and hatred for whomever it was who did this to my innocent child. Bible passages about God's giving His Son and the torture of Jesus helped but never completely eased my mind. Often at night I would slip into Daniel's room and sit by his bed, praying for God to heal him completely and restore him to the bright child he once was.

God answered my prayer—His answer was, "No. Trust Me."

The longer I struggled with God's negative reply, the more the waves of hatred and violence I felt for Danny's attackers were directed toward the Redeemer. Sometimes I told Christ, "I hate You!" I was never quite able to convince myself that it was true, but I felt the frustration and anger and hatred so desperately.

The body of believers was wonderful through it all. They *all* passed through our home within forty-eight hours after Danny's attack, slipping in and out quietly so as not to annoy the neighbors. When we cried, they cried. When we praised the King of heaven, they praised the King of heaven. Occasionally a burst of laughter would descend over us from heaven, working like an emotional safety valve. We would laugh clean and hearty laughs and be temporarily cleansed. We would sing.

The members of the body were family. No—*more* than family. They were *life,* living distributors of the only true life which kept us alive for the four remaining years. All our previous denominational and minor doctrinal differences had become blurred into loving unity.

Enraptured

I will never forget the greatest day of my Earth hour. I was heading home from work as the sun was easing near the horizon and reddish-orangish-purplish tones watercolored the clouds. Maria had arranged to have a few of Danny's friends over for a little birthday celebration.

The trauma in his life, while never forgotten, had faded somewhat into the grey draperies which sometimes decorate, sometimes obscure, the past. The hideous event and its results had been *accommodated* like we do with other forms of ugliness if we live with them long enough.

We had accommodated Danny's strangeness and disabilities. The increasingly all-consuming terrors of everyday life and the unconditional love we had for Danny

merged to make the past violence done to him "no big deal."
I had even accommodated — and with joy — God's terse "No.
Trust Me."

I glanced at my time chip and calculated I should arrive just in time to join the other party-goers. I pulled into
the driveway and hopped off my bicycle.

Suddenly there was an eerie silence in the atmosphere.
It was as if life had been suspended for a moment or two.
Then came the noise. At first I thought it was an
earthquake because it vibrated everything. But there was
something unusual. The sound caused the entire earth to
resonate. It had to be unlike any sound the earth had witnessed since angel battalions announced the birth of the
Messiah to a bunch of shepherds outside Bethlehem.

The volume was so great that it seemed like a modu-
lated atomic explosion. There were definitely words being
said. Though my body was paralyzed by fright, my mind
desperately tried to make out the words. They finally came:

"Announcing, O Earth, King Jesus; bow before Him!"

"Announcing, O Earth, King Jesus; bow before Him!"

"Announcing, O Earth, King Jesus; bow before Him!"

"Announcing, O Earth, King Jesus; bow before Him!"

The reverberations set my soul in motion. There was
something chilling, exciting, exhilarating about what was
happening. Fernando said he heard the words in Spanish.
Ching Lee heard them in Mandarin.

Then, over the top of the voice, came the brass.
Deafening. Like having someone blast his bugle directly
into your ear. Like 10,000 trumpets, coronets, trombones
and French horns in a celestial fanfare.

Against the darkening backdrop of the eastern sky

came a light. It started tiny, like a Star of Bethlehem, and got brighter and brighter as it grew in size. Like a combination of a welder's arc and a strobe light, it grew blinding as it pulsed rapidly. You couldn't stand to look at it as it filled the sky above the horizon and cast sharp shadows behind every item it struck. Yet you couldn't take your eyes off it either. I stood transfixed, unaware that there was anything or anyone else in the world but me.

Light of the World

Then, in the center of the light, I saw Him. I knew in an instant it was He. It wasn't His facial features. The radiance was too bright to see a face. It was just . . . it was just His presence, His aura, His countenance.

In that suspended moment my life passed before me like a video in "hyperscan" mode. Compressed into that millisecond was delight at the thousands of scenes of personal obedience, faith, love, giving, serving . . . then, on the flip side of that delight, I saw a fast-paced visual documentary of all the evil I had done. It was *horrendous*. The terrible overview of my lifetime sins created instant nausea.

My knees were beginning to buckle when suddenly my whole body felt light, lighter than air. My eyes still fixed on Him, and it seemed that I was drawing closer to Him. I sensed there were others beside me, but I could not bear to tear my eyes away from Him. Drawing closer now, I could see He was smiling graciously. My spirit, which had been in a whirlwind of turbulence, now grew strangely calm.

He isn't angry at me. He loves me, I thought as I observed the pure affection pouring from His eyes. We drew closer to each other. *He's forgiven me! He's* **forgiven** *me! He's forgiven* **me!** I thought as I drew within range of His outstretched arms.

Then His arms closed around me. I could feel His warmth and the strength of His embrace. His soft beard stroked my face and a tear from His eyes tickled my shoulder.

Together at last. Together at last! *We were together at last!*

"My son," He whispered with a warm chuckle, "My wonderful prodigal. Welcome to the feast."

Collective Affection

For the first time I noticed I was not alone. Maria was pressed next to me in that embrace . . . and Charity . . . and Danny. I looked twice, three times at Daniel. There was no hollow look in his eyes. His countenance was bright and his body completely restored like I had dreamed he would be if God would heal him. Daniel smiled at me and said softly, "He did it, Dad. He answered your prayers." We cried together. Charity and Maria wept with joy on each other's shoulders.

Tears continued to flow unrestrained even though we couldn't move. We were still pressed in that divine embrace together.

I then became aware of the tremendous noise around us. It was like break time at a great political convention. No, more like the joyful conversational buzz of an enormous wedding reception.

Who did I see then but *Mom*. It was my godly mother who I hadn't seen in years. She was in the embrace too. And Grandpa and Grandma. And our first church pastor. And my high school classmate who was killed in the war with China.

It was incredible. As I focused my eyes through the

tears which filled them, I could see the embrace growing to thousands, then millions, then maybe *hundreds of millions!* We all were close and intimate with our loving friend, yet we were so many. This was no occasion to try to figure out how this could be—this was a time to *enjoy.*

This was also no time to figure how we all got from earth to here. No time to wonder what was going on behind with those who were left. No time to look back like Lot's wife at Sodom. No time to complain or grieve or question. It was just a time to enjoy.

Feasting for the Family

Angelic hosts ushered us into the celestial banquet hall. The entrance to the ballroom looked a thousand feet high. The walls were made of pure white marble covered with decorative carvings inlaid with gold. The musical melodies of a thousand symphony orchestras wafted through the hundred-foot-high mahogany doors. The fragrance of delicate cooking spices and herbs announced to the senses, now strangely heightened and keen, that the Marriage Feast of the Lamb was about to begin. The unseen guest at the Passover was now fully visible, sitting right there at the right side of the Father.

What a grand celebration! At the dais stood the Father, the Son of Man and His Bride— all x hundreds of millions of us. How many I could never venture to guess. The Holy Spirit occupied and filled the million-acre banquet hall with His loving, gracious presence. The atmosphere was charged with exceedingly extravagant joy.

It had been worth it all.

In the nine hundred years since the day of deliverance I have learned many more of the "whys and wherefores." In informal conversations with the King we all have had our questions answered about things that occurred during our Earth hour. He has explained His righteous purposes for allowing us to suffer.

The King, reflecting on His own suffering and persecution on planet Earth, explained His perspective:

"My lovely bride, My Church, I know you suffered what you thought was much during my absence. Was it really much? Suppose I had given you the choice in the world to have your suffering spread over your entire earthly lifetime or to have it all condensed into one terrible hour never to suffer again — one hour of seventy-five years? What would you have chosen?"

We all declared, "One hour, O King!"

"You received less, my precious Church. You received one Earth hour of suffering and persecution out of an *eternal lifetime* in which you will never suffer again."

It was now all clear.

We praised Him. We sang to Him. We embraced Him once more.

And the celebration has never ceased.

God's promise of protection —
but the choice is yours

13
The Final Curtain

"When these things begin to take place, stand up and lift up
your heads, because your redemption is drawing near."

Jesus Christ
Luke 21:28

☐   ☐   ☐

Congratulations! You've made it to the last chapter.

We have journeyed together through the rising
fearstorm, into the world of biblical prophecy and through
the beginnings of the labor pains that will signify a time of
great persecution. We have examined scores of factors that
New Testament prophets declared would be marks of the
last generation. We have studied evidence of the changing
societal character we see around us today that predictive
literature has declared would mark the terminal society.
We have asked, "Where is the power of the Church of Jesus

Christ?" and we got a less than satisfactory answer.

We traversed back in time to 1947 and down into hell for a meeting of the Demonic High Council where we took notes on Lucifer's presentation of his Half-Century Plan. Then we checked to see if there is evidence that this plan is proceeding successfully. We considered ten responses to the rising persecution which should help us prepare for the full force of it. Nine of the directives were straight from the prophets who predicted the suffering and one was wisdom for effective parenting.

We traveled 900+ years into the future to hear the story of a man who described the last days from his ascended vantage point. We heard his happy ending as one of the "sheep" who got to meet the Good Shepherd personally as part of the bride of Christ whose wedding day and feasting time came.

What I Didn't Say

Yet there is so much I did not share.

I didn't even touch on the fifteen chapters of Revelation which detail even more hideous and outrageous happenings than those I outlined here. I didn't even mention the two great future wars in which the conquering Christ and His army of believers do battle with the nations of the world and with the forces of the dark side. I gave no description of the rise of a super man, inspired by Beelzebub, or of his global control of a one-world government.

I did not so much as hint at the great White Throne judgment, pictured for John by the Holy Spirit as a time when every human individual dead or alive has his name checked against the records to see if he qualifies for future rewards or deserves everlasting punishment. I didn't describe the Heavenly City, a 1500-mile "cubic condominium" promised as a dwelling place to those whose names are found written in the "Lamb's Book of Life."

And there are many more wonderful things promised to the faithful believers in Christ, but to mention them all would probably take dozens of books!

The Curtain Is Closing

The curtain is now closing on this particular book, one man's perspective told from his heart and his head and based on the teaching of the book of books.

All the evidence amassed here, and untold volumes of data far beyond the scope of coverage in this book, say we are facing the end of an era. Jesus said of this time:

> When these things begin to take place, stand up and lift up your heads, because your redemption is drawing near . . . Look at the fig tree and all the trees. When they sprout leaves, you can see for yourselves and know that summer is near. Even so, when you see these things happening, you know that the kingdom of God is near.[1]

One doesn't have to be Sherlock Holmes to figure out what season is coming when trees sprout. Jesus' reference is straightforward in saying, in essence, that only a dummy could miss the signs of the second coming of Jesus Christ. (I told you I would get back to this.)

Our futuristic friend in the previous chapter described his encounter with Jesus on what he called the day of deliverance. I based that description on the following prophecy written by the apostle Paul in a letter to Christians in Thessaloniki (the modern name), Greece:

> For the Lord himself will come down from Heaven with a loud command, with the voice of the archangel and

with the trumpet call of God, and the dead in Christ will rise first. After that, we who are still alive and are left will be caught up with them in the clouds to meet the Lord in the air. And so we will be with the Lord forever. Therefore, encourage each other with these words.[2]

Sounds like an opening *curtain to me, Larry,* you're probably thinking. *Why is the heading of this section called, "The Curtain Is Closing"?*

One simple reason. The voice from heaven shouting and the trumpet blowing to announce Christ's return are the "final curtain." It will be the last chance for anyone to make a decision to trust Him. *One second* after that there will be no more opportunities to be included in His fabulous free offer of forgiveness, spiritual power, abundant life, a 100-fold ROI (return on investment) for everything suffered on earth and eternal life as a bonus. After that it's "Sorry, Charlie!"

Isn't that a dirty deal?

Are you kidding? A "dirty deal" after God has given us *2000 or more years* to anticipate the timing of the final curtain and scores of prophetic signs that are all lining up to declare that the curtain is about to close? And now that you have all the information in this book for which you are accountable, you'd better be *really* sure this decision is settled. Now.

If you want to turn down Christ's offer, then you "pays your money and makes your choice." But I want to assure you that this is *not* God's desire for you. Want to hear what His desires for you are? They can be summarized in three statements, the first from the apostle Paul addressing the sheep:

For God did not appoint us to suffer wrath but to receive salvation through our Lord Jesus Christ. He died for us so that, whether we are awake or asleep, we may live together with him.[3]

The second statement is from the writer of Hebrews, addressed to the goats:

> You have come to God, the Judge of all men, to the spirits of righteous men made perfect, to Jesus the mediator of a new contract . . . *See to it that you do not refuse Him who speaks.* If they did not escape when they refused Him who warned them on earth, how much less will we, if we turn away from Him who warns us from Heaven [emphasis added]?[4]

The third statement is from Peter, addressed "To Whom It May Concern":

> But do not forget this one thing, dear friends: With the Lord a day is like a thousand years and a thousand years are like a day. The Lord is not slow in keeping His promise, as some understand slowness. He is *patient with you, not wanting anyone to perish* but everyone to come to repentance [emphasis added].[5]

Sheep or Goat?

If your name is "Billy" or "Nanny," I plead with you, get into the sheep category *now* before the final curtain closes.

If your name is "Baa-Baa," it's time *now* to get out of the black sheep category and get back into the fold with the shepherd who loved you so much He gave His life for you and the rest of us animals.

How do I do that, Larry?

Thought you'd never ask.

Below you'll find a prayer that asks God to take control of your life. Read it through to see if it is the kind of prayer you'd like to pray. The words certainly aren't magical; you can express the thoughts in your own words if you like.

If the prayer seems like one you'd like to pray, pray it out loud so you can hear yourself praying it, okay?

Dear God, I realize I have been ignoring a lot of signs You've been giving me, signs designed to get my attention and bring me into a close relationship with You before the opportunity is gone. Here I am. I surrender.

I confess the many things I have done that I know displease You. Please forgive me. Lord Jesus, I place my trust in You as my rescuer. I give You control of my life right now.

Give me supernatural power to be the kind of person You want me to be regardless of what challenges I may face.

Thank You for hearing my prayer and answering it. I gratefully accept Your free gift of eternal life.

Amen.

Now take a deep breath and think about what you just prayed. Great feeling, isn't it? God bless you. I trust you will never be the same.

Telling a Book by Its Cover

Before we part, would you take just one moment and look at the front cover of this book, the picture *behind* the words?

The artist captured beautifully a scene taken from the

book of the Revelation, a portrait of the four horses of the Apocalypse. This scene, set in the midst of the worst horror the world will ever know, the dreaded Great Tribulation, signifies one dimension of the outpouring of God's wrath on all those who have stubbornly resisted His grace and patience for millennia.

Based on the information given in Revelation Chapter 6, I interpret this scene as follows:

- The *white horse* represents the combined power of church and state which Satan's "only begotten son," the antichrist, will ride to conquer the nations and establish his one-world order.

- The *red horse* represents the blood and fire of the wars fought by the antichrist, leaving death and destruction far worse than any war before in human history.

- The *black horse* represents the suffering and death resulting from the failure of the antichrist's global economic system, resulting in "a quart of wheat costing a whole day's wage."

- The *pale horse* represents the suffering resulting from famines, plagues and marauding wild animals, the final desperate state of the earth after the ascendancy of the second person of the unholy trinity.

In the cover artwork, unlike the scene in Revelation, the horses have no riders. God has untied the steeds on which the terrible occult conquerors will ride *with His permission* to bring judgment on evil men and nations. But the riders are yet to be revealed.

When the riders from the pits of hell are saddled and mounted, you won't want to be around. If you have placed your trust in the living Christ, even as recently as ten paragraphs ago, you are in His protection. He will protect you *from* or protect you *through* anything that comes your way.

Jesus Himself promised:

> You will be betrayed even by parents, brothers, relatives, and friends, and they will put some of you to death. All men will hate you because of me. But *not a hair of your head will perish.* By standing firm you will gain life.[6]

The decision to trust in Him, then, above all else, is absolutely the single most significant thing you can do to prepare for the coming persecution.

By standing firm, you will gain life!

Appendix A

Biblical Background for Satan's "Half-Century Plan"

While the scene in Chapter 9 of Satan addressing the Demonic High Council is obviously a fantasy scenario, it is rooted firmly in biblical revelation. Below you'll find biblical passages which support key concepts of Lucifer's presentation.

1. Theron's oversight of Europe is based on the fact that demons have been given oversight over geographical/national areas (Daniel 10:12,13 – the prince of Persia mentioned here is symbolic of a demon).

2. Domni's involvement in the Holocaust demonstrates that demons delight in torturing human beings (Luke 8:26-29 and Mark 9:17-22).

3. Destroying a democracy by destroying moral consensus comes from the principle that righteousness exalts a nation but degenerate character destroys it (Proverbs 14:34 with Leviticus 18:24-28).

4. Satan's future control of the financial system is described in Revelation 13:16-18.

5. The disastrous consequences of a nation relying on its military might is described in Isaiah 31:1-5.

6. The moral consequences of individualism and divisiveness is shown in James 3:16.

7. The multi-generational consequences of sin in families is taught in Exodus 20:5, thus making the corruption of the biblical family model a powerful strategy.

8. Under Satan's influence, modern media violates the command of Scripture to make sure our thought processes are directed toward things that are pure and noble (Philippians 4:8,9).

9. Sexual impurity, especially homosexuality, represents God's "turning over" a person to Satan's evil influence present in his life (Romans 1:24-27).

10. The story of David's playing music for King Saul illustrates the principle that music has a powerful effect on the human spirit (1 Samuel 16:14-23).

11. Satan's "only begotten son" coming to earth is described in Revelation 13:1b-7.

12. That the destruction will come on the earth at a time when "peace and safety" are being proclaimed is taught in 1 Thessalonians 5:1-3.

13. The antichrist and false prophet will do mighty miracles to authenticate their "messiahship" according to Revelation 13:2b-4,12-14.

14. Revelation 13:7,8 tells us that the antichrist will unite all the world's nations into one world government and religion.

15. That Christians will be neutralized in their effectiveness in the last days is seen in the description of the last church of seven historic churches, Laodicea, which is "lukewarm" (Revelation 3:14-18).

16. That civilization will be partying to such an extent that the impending end-time disaster will escape their notice is taught in Matthew 24:36-41.

17. Satan's "unholy spirit," dwelling in a supernaturally powerful false prophet, or "second beast," is described in Revelation 13:11-15.

18. The death and resurrection of Satan's "son," the antichrist, is described in Revelation 13:3,12,14.

19. Satan's deception is so cunning that even believers in Christ would be deceived but for Christ's supernatural illumination according to Matthew 24:24.

20. Revelation 13:4 declares that no one will dare stand against the powerful antichrist.

Appendix B

Biblical Background for the Nature of Christ's Second Coming

While the scene in Chapter 12 of the unnamed man being transported into the air to meet Christ is obviously a fantasy scenario, it is rooted firmly in biblical revelation. In this appendix you'll find biblical passages which support key concepts of that man's experience, an experience declared to be that of all believers in Jesus Christ (1 Corinthians 15:50-57).

1. The sound of a loud, heavenly voice accompanying Christ's return in the air is declared in 1 Thessalonians 4:16.

2. The sound of a loud trumpet call accompanying Christ's return in the air is also declared in 1 Thessalonians 4:16.

3. Every person in the universe will be called to bow to Jesus Christ according to Philippians 2:9-11.

4. That Christ's persona is like a glorious, bright radiance is taught in Revelation 1:14,16; 21:23,24.

5. Revelation 20:11-15 teaches that the deeds of men will be the basis for their evaluation unless they have their name written in the Lamb's Book of Life.

6. Believers alive at Christ's return will rise from earth to meet Christ in the air according to 1 Thessalonians 4:17a.

7. First Thessalonians 4:16b says that deceased believers will rise to meet Christ in the air.

8. That believers caught up in the air will be in the presence of Christ from that time on forever is taught in 1 Thessalonians 4:17b.

9. Believers in Christ, though having sinned, will enter the presence of Christ forgiven based on 1 John 1:9,10 and Romans 8:1-5.

10. That believers in great multitudes will be in attendance at a marriage feast after their arrival in the presence of Christ is described in Revelation 19:6-9.

11. Suffering for the believer is brief and minuscule compared to the glory of eternal life according to Romans 8:17,18.

12. That even accidents will be providentially prevented in the new kingdom is taught in Isaiah 65:20-23 (compare with Psalm 91:9-11).

DISCUSSION GUIDE

for Group Study of

THE COMING PERSECUTION

**by the editors of
Here's Life Publishers**

SESSION 1

Chapter 1: The Fearstorm
Chapter 2: Twenty (Loaded) Questions

1. When you first saw the title and cover of this book, *The Coming Persecution*, what inner feelings made you want to read it?

2. Columnist Tom Wicker calls our era "The Age of Apprehension." Author Larry Poland calls it a "fearstorm" that is unique to our generation. In what areas of our culture have you observed increasing levels of fear and apprehension?

3. Read 2 Timothy 3:1 at the beginning of Chapter 1. What dynamics do you feel make this prophetic time period "terrifying"?

4. As a group, go through the twenty questions posed by the author in Chapter 2. Explain your answers, giving examples from current events or recent personal experiences.

5. The author asks, "Could it be that things are turning against Christians on a global scale?" What do you think?

SESSION 2

Chapter 3: Piercing the Veil

1. The author recalls a personal experience which, to him, went far beyond mere "coincidence." Can you remember a set of circumstances in your own life which you feel could only have been "engineered" by Divine Intelligence?

2. What do such experiences tell us about the sovereignty of God over personal, national and world developments?

   If God were to tell us of an incredible set of circumstances that will come together in the near future, how should we respond?

3. Think about some of the predictions you have seen in the headlines of supermarket tabloids. Can you think of any that came true?

   Can you think of some that have not?

4. What was the criterion God gave Moses for determining whether a prophet was trustworthy? (See Deuteronomy 18:17-21.)

   Why do you suppose His standards were so high?

   What does Moses' criterion tell us about whose predictions we should trust?

5. Jesus Christ Himself fulfilled more than 300 Old Testament prophecies about His coming. Then, in His own ministry, Jesus made several specific predictions about the end times, which the apostle Paul later expanded upon. Do you think we can count on these prophecies coming true? If so, why?

SESSION 3
Chapter 4: Labor Pains

1. Read Matthew 24:4-8 together. Why do you suppose Jesus used the analogy of "beginning birth pains" to describe what would take place near the end of the age?

2. Chapter 4 details five specific prophecies made by Jesus, Jude, Peter and Paul, which Jesus called the "the beginning of birth pains." Giving specific examples, discuss whether you have noticed the following in our world today:

   a. A significant and widespread increase in famines.

   b. A significant and widespread increase in earthquakes.

   c. A dramatic increase in the number of phony "messiahs."

   d. A radical increase in national and ethnic wars and war rumors.

   e. A predominance of intellectual and religious scoffers who ridicule the notion of the waning era of man or of any impending catastrophe.

3. Of course, all of the above signs have existed at one time or another throughout history. But the author believes that these five prophecies have now converged on actual human events as never before. After reading Chapter 4, do you agree? Why or why not?

   If the author is right, what do you think it means for our generation?

4. What good things could God bring about in our lives by allowing such difficult times?

SESSION 4

Chapter 5: A Good Man Is Harder to Find

1. Review the first five "beginning birth pains" discussed in Chapter 4. Have any news events or personal experiences taken place since the last session that would seem to fit in with one of these five predictions?

2. The apostle Paul shares a sixth "beginning birth pain" in 2 Timothy 3:12,13. Read these verses, then discuss the question the author poses at the start of Chapter 5: "Do you ever get this strange feeling that the collective morality of those in the world around you is deteriorating?" Give examples to support your answers.

3. Second Timothy 3:12,13 actually summarizes a detailed listing of twenty-one indicators of end-time corruption that Paul predicted in the same chapter of this letter. For the sake of clarity, the author of *The Coming Persecution* has "repackaged" these into seventeen indicators (discussed over Chapters 5, 6, 7 and 8 of this book) to help us examine the sixth "beginning birth pain" in detail. Read 2 Timothy 3:1-5 together. How do you think God will feel when He observes these types of people dominating His creation?

4. Chapter 5 examines the first two of these seventeen indicators of end-time corruption. Share some examples of how you have observed society to be

   Lovers of themselves . . .

   Lovers of money . . .

5. Are Christians exempt from becoming lovers of self and lovers of money? What are some of the subtle ways we can fall into these traps?

SESSION 5

Chapter 6: Is It <u>Ever</u> Hard to Find a Good Man!

1. In Chapter 6 the author examines four more of Paul's seventeen indicators of the moral decline of man. From your personal observations, or from Chapter 6, cite a telling example of how today's citizenry tends to be

   Lovers of pleasure rather than lovers of God . . .

   Not lovers of the good . . .

   Boastful, proud . . .

   Without love.

2. Do you feel that today's Christians also fall into these patterns? In what ways?

3. Have you ever caught yourself falling into these patterns? Can you share an example that would be helpful to the others in your group?

4. What would you tell a dedicated Christian who asks, "How can I learn from my mistakes and stand strong when I'm tempted

   to love pleasure more than God . . .

   to pursue evil things . . .

   to be boastful or proud . . .

   to be unloving?"

5. The author acknowledges that "to be indicating marks of an *historically unique generation*," Paul's seventeen characteristics would have to differ from those of previous generations in two dimensions: (1) the evil would have to be more extreme than ever before, and (2) acceptance and practice of the evil would have to be significantly wider than ever before. Do you feel that with the six indicators studied thus far, today's generation might meet the criteria? Why?

SESSION 6

Chapter 7: The Bad Guy Glut

1. By now you may be thinking, *Enough already! Looking at all this negative stuff is depressing!* You're right, it's not pleasant. Why do you think Jesus, Jude, Peter and Paul went to the effort to spell out specific marks of the end times for us?

   In what ways can this knowledge benefit us?

   In what ways will this knowledge benefit the work of God on our planet?

   Does God want us to react with fear when we learn these things? How do you think He wants us to respond?

2. In Chapter 7 the author continues our examination of Paul's seventeen predictions regarding man's moral decline in the last days. (These indicators are a detailed look at the sixth "beginning birth pain" referred to in Chapters 4 and 5.) Together, read 2 Timothy 3:1-5, 13. From Chapter 7 of *The Coming Persecution*, share a point of evidence that stands out to you (or a personal observation you've made this week) about how today's society tends to be more

   slanderous . . .

   rash . . .

   brutal . . .

   disobedient to parents . . .

   treacherous . . .

   deceitful.

3. As we Christians observe these negative things taking place around us, how should we then live? Why?

4. What positive action steps can we take as Christians to share God's love with a hurting people?

5. At this point in our study, how do you feel about the possibility that we could be in the very generation Paul was speaking of?

SESSION 7

Chapter 8: Fizzled Fission

1. In Chapter 8 the author wraps up our look at the apostle Paul's seventeen predictions regarding the last-days decline of the character of man. Dr. Poland believes these last five indicators describe a "perverse religion" that will creep into society to dissipate the power of our faith. From Chapter 8, share a point of evidence that stands out to you (or a personal observation you've made recently) about how society in general (and Christians in particular) might be becoming more

   ungrateful . . .

   unholy . . .

   unforgiving . . .

   without self-control . . .

   having a form of godliness but denying its power.

2. Have you ever caught yourself falling into these patterns of behavior? Can you share an example that would be helpful to the others in your group?

3. At the start of Chapter 8, the author describes a personal experience in which a group of believers was spiritually impotent due to unresolved sin and conflict. By humbling themselves before God, they were restored to love, fellowship and spiritual power. What lessons can we draw from such experiences?

   Would you like to pray as a group for the kind of spiritual life and power experienced in this example?

4. After reading the first eight chapters of our study, what conclusions or convictions have you sensed God is forming in your heart about your lifestyle? Your attitude? Your walk with God?

SESSION 8

Chapter 9: Satan's Half-Century Plan

1. Read aloud the quote from *The Screwtape Letters* at the beginning of Chapter 9. Can you think of some ways in which C. S. Lewis's fictional account may actually be coming true today?

2. In this chapter, the author creates a fantasy scenario of Lucifer presenting his Half-Century Plan to the Demonic High Council in 1947. Beginning with POLITICS on page 129 and ending with THE ARTS on page 131, have group members read aloud each category of the plan. After each of the categories, pause and discuss the question, "In what ways have these strategies actually become reality during the past five decades?" (Refer to Appendix A for related Scriptures.)

3. Lucifer's final strategy (page 133) is to unleash his own substitute for Christianity. Read this section aloud, then read the Scripture predicting this event listed in Appendix A. What events and attitudes have you observed in our culture that could be paving the way for society's acceptance of such a "messiah" from Satan?

4. As you read about the different types of Heavy Metal rock music that exist in our culture today, what stood out to you as

   something that surprised you . . .

   something to talk to your kids about . . .

   something to pray about . . .

   something on which to take a stand?

5. In the midst of all the turmoil in our world, do you believe that dedicated Christians can still live a life of joy and hope? Explain your answer.

SESSION 9

Chapter 10: Into the Black Hole

1. Read Luke 21:6-17. Do you think the scenario Jesus describes could possibly happen in our lifetime, in our culture? Explain your answer.

2. In Chapter 10, the author cites several examples of how committed Christians have recently been publicly demeaned, harassed, or discriminated against for taking a stand for Judeo-Christian principles. Which example stood out to you the most? Why?

3. Can you think of other recent happenings in our country in which public sentiment has generally been one of disdain for Christians and what we believe in? Consider these areas:

   Schools: what can and cannot be taught . . .

   Churches: where they can and cannot meet; how they can and cannot raise necessary funds . . .

   Social issues: abortion, sexual attitudes . . .

   Politics: Christian convictions in government . . .

   Media: free speech vs. responsible speech . . .
   good taste vs. censorship . . .
   media's perception and representation of evangelical Christians . . .

4. As we Christians observe these scenarios unfolding around us in real life, how should we respond

   Privately (our attitude and prayer life)?

   Among our families (our attitude and our nurturing of others)?

   Publicly (our attitude and countenance, and our actions)?

5. In light of the increasing hostility toward dedicated Christians, what type of commitment do you sense God is asking you to make to Him, to your family, and to your fellow Christians right now?

SESSION 10

Chapter 11: Don't Worry, Be Happy!

1. Read Matthew 25:31-46. Here Jesus describes the day of judgment in which God will separate the "sheep" from the "goats." Into which category do you think He will place individuals who uphold His standards during persecution? Explain your answer.

2. The author shares ten positive strategies to help Christians be spiritually, physically, mentally and emotionally prepared for the tough days ahead. Divide the study group equally and assign each one or two individuals a strategy. Give the groups five minutes to review their sections, then have them summarize for the rest of the group the practical and scriptural advice the author gives.

    After each strategy has been summarized, discuss briefly: "How will this strategy help you stand strong when it's not popular to be a Christian?" "What is one practical thing you can begin doing this week to implement the author's advice?"

3. Why can believers rejoice in the midst of heartache, pain and persecution?

4. What are three action steps you can take to stay positive and strong whenever you find yourself getting fearful or discouraged?

SESSION 11
Chapter 12: Glory, Glory, Hallelujah!

1. In this book, the author has purposefully refrained from an argument on when the Rapture of believers will occur. But he believes that regardless of how the Rapture or the Great Tribulation fall into place, Christians in our culture will be subjected to increasing disdain, hostility and persecution before then. Have some of the evidences in this book convinced you he might be right? Which ones stood out to you?

2. Chapter 12 is a dramatic fantasy scenario in which an unnamed man, writing from heaven some 900 + years in the future, tells of his final days on Earth before being caught up to meet Jesus Christ in the clouds. Before your group gets together, appoint a good reader to give a dramatic reading of the chapter while the group follows along. Then discuss, "What emotions did you feel as we were going through this chapter?" "What emotions did you feel at the end?"

3. How did Christians help one another survive during the open persecution in this story? What ideas come to you of how we can encourage and help one another as times grow tougher?

4. Read Revelation 21:1-8. As you read this passage of prophetic scripture, what specific promises are especially meaningful to you?

5. Read aloud the King's speech to His children on the last page of Chapter 12 and imagine that He is saying these words directly to you. What new perspective does this give you regarding difficulty you may face in your time here on Earth?

SESSION 12

Chapter 13: The Final Curtain

1. Read Luke 21:19-36. In the midst of all the signs Jesus provides to indicate that we may be in the last days, what positive promises does He make?

   What positive action steps does He exhort us to take?

2. Through His New Testament writers, God gives special messages to the faithful and to the unfaithful regarding His desire for them when Christ returns. Read aloud 1 Thessalonians 5:9-11, Hebrews 12:23-26, and 2 Peter 3:8,9. After each passage, discuss:

   Is the writer addressing the faithful or the unfaithful?

   What is His expressed desire for the people to whom He speaks?

3. How can a person be absolutely sure that "whether we are awake or asleep, we may live together with Him?"

4. Read Paul's description of the return of Christ in 1 Thessalonians 4:16-18. Notice that he commands believers to "encourage each other with these words." In what way are these words encouraging to followers of Christ? How can believers obey Paul's command today?

5. In what ways has your study of *The Coming Persecution* been helpful to you?

6. Read 2 Peter 3:10-13. Discuss Peter's question: "What kind of people ought you to be?" Do you feel any changes in your life are now necessary as a result of reading *The Coming Persecution?* Why or why not? What steps will have to be taken to bring about these changes?

7. Can you think of family and friends who should read *The Coming Persecution?*

Notes

Chapter One

1. Tom Wicker, "Fear Itself," *Vogue* (January 1984), pp. 172, 256.
2. Sylvia Nasar, "The $2 Trillion Debt Headache," *Fortune* (November 10, 1986), pp. 42-48.
3. Mortimer B. Zuckerman, "Brother, Can You Spare a Dime?" *U. S. News and World Report* (August 22, 1988).
4. Zuckerman, "Brother, Can You Spare a Dime?"
5. *Crime in the United States: Uniform Crime Reports* (Washington, D.C.: Federal Bureau of Investigation, 1989), p. 19.
6. David L. Kirp and Steven Epstein, "AIDS in America's Schoolhouses: Learning the Hard Lessons," *Phi Delta Kappan* (April 1989), pp. 585-593.
7. Bruce Ritter, *God Has a Kid's Face* (New York: Covenent House, 1988).
8. *Los Angeles Times* (May 20, 1989).
9. Roger J. Magnuson, *Are Gay Rights Right?* (Minneapolis: Straitgate Press, 1985), p. 17.
10. "Downfall of a Neighborhood," *Life* (July 1988), pp. 93-100.
11. *McAlvaney Intelligence Advisor* (July 1989).
12. 2 Timothy 3:1, NIV.
13. Luke 21:26, NIV.

Chapter Three

1. 1 Corinthians 2:9,10 and Romans 8:14, NIV.
2. Deuteronomy 18:17-21, NIV.
3. Josh McDowell, *Evidence That Demands a Verdict* (San Bernardino, CA: Here's Life Publishers, 1972), pp. 150-184.
4. Revelation 13:16,17, NIV.
5. Revelation 11:8,9, NIV.

Chapter Four

1. Matthew 24:8, NIV.
2. These are taken from Matthew 24:3-8, Jude 18,19, 2 Peter 3:2-9 and 2 Timothy 3:1-9.
3. "Famine," *The World Book Encyclopedia* (Chicago: World Book, Inc., 1989), p. 28.
4. "Famine," p. 28.
5. "Report of the Lausanne Congress on World Evangelism Statistics Task Force

to the Lausanne II Congress," D. B. Barrett Statistics Coordinator, 1989.

6. John W. Helmuth, "World Hunger Amidst Plenty," *USA Today* (March 1989), p. 48.

7. "Major Earthquakes," *The World Almanac and Book of Facts* (New York: Pharos Books, 1989), p. 524.

8. "Major Earthquakes," p. 524.

9. "Major Earthquakes," p. 524.

10. Dave Hunt, *Peace, Prosperity, and the Coming Holocaust* (Eugene, OR: Harvest House Publishers, 1983), pp. 85-97.

11. Dave Hunt, *Peace, Prosperity, and the Coming Holocaust*, p. 89.

12. Ruth Montgomery, *A Gift of Prophecy: The Phenomenal Jeanne Dixon* (New York: n.p., 1965), p. 172.

13. Matthew 24:5, NIV.

14. 2 Peter 3:3,4, TLB.

15. 2 Peter 3:3,4, TLB.

16. Jude 18,19, NIV.

17. 1 Thessalonians 5:1-3, NIV.

Chapter Five

1. 2 Timothy 3:12,13, NIV.

2. 2 Timothy 3:1-7, NIV.

3. "Growing Pains at 40," *Time* (May 19, 1986), p. 37.

4. "The Death of Social Conscience," *Mademoiselle* (December 1987), p. 124.

5. Jane O'Reilly, "Three Faces of Greed," *Vogue* (August 1985), p. 199.

6. "Greed Gains Ground," *U. S. News and World Report* (January 25, 1988), p. 10.

7. Robert J. Ringer, *Looking Out for #1* (New York: Funk and Wagnalls, 1977), p. 2.

8. Robert J. Ringer, p. 10.

9. Michael Korda, *Success!* (New York: Random House, 1977), p. 4.

10. Michael Korda, p. 13.

11. "Personal Bankruptcies Accelerating," *The McAlvany Intelligence Advisor* (September 1989), p. 9.

12. Ezra Bowen, "What Ever Became of Honest Abe?" *Time* (April 4, 1988), p. 68.

13. "Morality Among the Supply-Siders," *Time* (May 25, 1987), pp. 19-20.

14. "Fraud, Fraud, Fraud," *Time* (August 15, 1988), p. 28.

15. "How to Rob a Bank Without a Gun," *Time* (August 15, 1988), p. 30.

16. "Tax Panel Says Business Doesn't Report Full Income," *Wall Street Journal* (October 18, 1988), p. B12.

17. David Cook, "Tax-cheat Rationale: Unfair IRS," *Christian Science Monitor*

(April 18, 1985), p. A1.

18. Daniel Coleman, "The Tax Cheats: Selfish to the Bottom Line," *New York Times* (April 11, 1988), pp. A1,D2.

Chapter Six

1. 2 Timothy 3:12,13, NIV.

2. *World Almanac and Book of Facts* (New York: Pharos Books, 1989), p. 593.

3. Don Richardson, *Peace Child* (Glendale, CA: G. L. Publications, 1974), p. 177.

4. Bob Emmers, "Film on Jesus Tempts Group to Boycott," *Orange County Register* (July 15, 1988), p. B1.

5. Matthew 24:12, NIV.

6. Douglas Martin, "Kitty Genovese: Would New York Still Turn Away?" *New York Times* (March 11, 1989), p. 29.

7. "Modern Man Remains the Wildest Animal," *U. S. News and World Report* (December 19, 1983), p. 54.

8. Malachi 2:13-16, NIV.

9. Carl Avery, "How Do You Build Intimacy in an Age of Divorce?" *Psychology Today* (Date needed), pp. 27-31.

10. Connel Cowan and Melvyn Kinder, "Fear of Intimacy: Not for Men Only," *Glamour* (October 1987), p. 96.

11. Judith Wallerstein, "Children After Divorce," *New York Times Magazine* (January 22, 1989), pp. 20-21.

12. Janet G. Woititz, *Adult Children of Alcoholics* (Pompano Beach, FL: Health Communicatsion, 1983).

13. Dr. Ken Magid and Carole A. McKelvey, *High Risk—Children Without a Conscience* (New York: Bantam Books, 1987), p. 67.

14. Dr. Ken Magid and Carole A. McKelvey, p. 67.

Chapter Seven

1. Sam Janus, *The Death of Innocence* (New York: William Morrow and Co., 1981), pp. 123-124.

2. George Hackett, "Kids: Deadly Force," *Newsweek* (January 11, 1988), pp. 18-19.

3. "Woman Fatally Hit by Gang Gunfire," *Los Angeles Times* (February 1, 1988), p. Ill.

4. "Fun Killers Now Paying Devil's Dues," *Los Angeles Times* (October 20, 1988), p. I23.

5. "Crime in Cities Outruns Police," *Los Angeles Times* (August 28, 1989), p. I14.

6. "Epidemic of Violence," *Scientific American* (October 1985), p. 85.

7. "Victims of Crime," *U. S. News and World Report* (July 31, 1989), p. 16.

8. Ted Gest, "These Perilous Halls of Learning," *U.S. News and World Report*

(March 13, 1989), pp. 68-69.

9. "Boy Shoots Fellow Student During Seige in Anaheim," *The San Bernardino County Sun* (October 6, 1989), p. I1.

10. *Statistical Abstract of the United States, 1989* (U. S. Department of Commerce), p. 172.

11. Sam Janus, p. 120.

12. Fern Eckman, "Battered Women," *McCalls* (November 1987), p. 157.

13. Luke 21:16, NIV.

14. These translations appear in the King James Version.

15. "World War II: Part 3, Desperate Years," *Time* (September 4, 1989), p. 29.

16. For the complete story of the controversy surrounding Universal Pictures release of *The Last Temptation of Christ,* see Larry Poland's book, *The Last Temptation of Hollywood* (Highland, CA: Mastermedia International, 1988).

17. 2 Timothy 3:13, NIV.

Chapter Eight

1. 2 Timothy 3:2, NIV.

2. Romans 1:21, NIV.

3. Lancelot Law Whyte, *The Universe of Experience* (New York: Harper and Row, 1974), p. 6.

4. Quoted in Dave Hunt, *The Cult Explosion* (Irvine, CA: Harvest House, 1980), p. 106.

5. Armand M. Nicholi II, "The Fractured Family: Following It Into the Future," *Christianity Today* (May 25, 1979), pp. 10-15.

6. See Exodus 22:19; Leviticus 18:23-30, 20:15; Deuteronomy 27:21.

7. Leviticus 18:24-30.

8. Roger Magnuson, *Are Gay Rights Right?* (Minneapolis: Straitgate Press, 1985), p. 14.

9. Roger Magnuson, *Are Gay Rights Right?* p. 14.

10. Sam Jones, *The Death of Innocence* (New York: William Morrow and Co., 1981), pp. 174, 178.

11. Alfie Kohn, "Shattered Innocence," *Psychology Today* (February 1987), p. 55*ff.*

12. "43% of Teens in Conservative Churches Have Sexual Relations by 18, Poll Finds," *Los Angeles Times* (February 6, 1988).

13. Paraphrase of 2 Timothy 3:5.

Chapter Nine

1. C. S. Lewis, *Screwtape Letters* (New York: Macmillan Company, 1943), p. 39.

2. Matthew 24:36-41, NIV.

3. "Teenagers and Sex Crimes," *Time* (June 5, 1989), p. 60.

4. Dave Hart, "Heavy Metal Madness," *Media Update* (July/August 1989),

pp. 1-5.

5. Frank York, "Rescuing the Devil's Teenagers," *Focus on the Family Citizen* (October 1989), p. 7.

6. Frank York, "Rescuing the Devil's Teenagers," p. 7.

7. Frank York, "Rescuing the Devil's Teenagers," p. 7.

8. Dianne Klein, "Satanic Sleuths," *Los Angeles Times* (May 25, 1989), p. V/1ff.

9. Dianne Klein, "Satanic Sleuths," p. 12.

10. Frank York, "Rescuing the Devil's Teenagers," p. 7.

11. Timothy K. Jones, "The Tax Exempt Witch," *Christianity Today* (October 6, 1989), p. 15.

Chapter Ten

1. These figures cannot be added together. One nation may possess more than one of the attributes recorded.

2. David B. Barrett, "Nairobi," *World Christian Encyclopedia* (New York: Oxford University Press, 1982), p. 5.

3. "Preview," *Los Angeles Times* (September 1, 1989), part VI, p. 12.

4. Daniel J. Popeo, *Not OUR America . . . the ACLU Exposed* (Washington D. C.: Washington Legal Foundation, 1989), pp. 91-92.

5. J. Shelby Sharpe, "The Coming Nuclear Attack on Christianity in America," *The Chalcedon Report,* #291 (October 1989), p. 2.

6. Serge Schmemman, "For Germany's Jews, The Night Hope Died," *New York Times* (November 8, 1988), p. A1/10.

7. "For Operation Rescue Pittsburgh Is Really 'The Pits!' " *Letter From Plymouth Rock* (Marlborough, NH: Publication of the Plymouth Rock Foundation, June 1989), p. 3.

8. Joseph Farah, "Hollywood's Ugly Anti-Christian Bigotry," *Between the Lines* (Vol. 2, No. 9), p. 1.

9. "Racketeering Charges Applied to Rescuers," *Gammon and Grange Nonprofit, Religious Liberties Newsletter* (April-May-June 1989), p. 7.

10. "Operation Rescue and 12 Activists Found in Contempt of Court," *National and International Religion Report* (September 11, 1989), p. 4.

Chapter Eleven

1. Matthew 25:31-46, NIV.

2. Luke 21:34,35, NIV.

3. Matthew 11:30, NIV.

4. Luke 21:36, NIV.

5. 1 Thessalonians 5:2,3, NIV.

6. Matthew 24:6b, NIV.

7. 2 Timothy 1:7, NIV.

8. Matthew 24:23-28, NIV.
9. 2 Timothy 3:6,7, NIV.
10. Matthew 24:17,18, NIV.
11. Matthew 24:46-51, NIV.
12. Luke 21:28, NIV.
13. Matthew 24:13, NIV.
14. Ephesians 6:13,14, NIV.
15. Luke 21:12, NIV.
16. Luke 21:14,15, NIV.
17. 2 Peter 3:10-12a, NIV.
18. Jude 18-21, NIV.
19. Proverbs 22:15, personal paraphrase
20. Luke 6:22,23, NIV.
21. Matthew 19:29, NIV.

Chapter Thirteen

1. Luke 21:28-31, NIV.
2. 1 Thessalonians 4:16-18, NIV.
3. 1 Thessalonians 5:9,10, NIV.
4. Hebrews 12:23-26, NIV.
5. 2 Peter 3:8,9, NIV.
6. Luke 21:16-19, NIV.

Acknowledgments

Many thanks to . . .

Les Stobbe, Dan Benson and Barb Sherrill of Here's Life Publishers for their wise and insightful counsel and encouragement;

my faithful researcher Jim Vincent;

the elders of Trinity Evangelical Free Church for their support of this time-consuming effort;

the staff of Mastermedia International for their accommodation of this project in my ministry schedule;

my family who had to go without a husband and father during the hundreds of hours I sat at a computer;

the most important person in my life, Jesus Christ, whom to know is life eternal.

FULL-COLOR POSTER

A beautiful full-color poster featuring the artwork from the front cover of **The Coming Persecution** is now available for your personal enjoyment.

Display this powerful artwork in:

- Sunday school classrooms
- Group Bible studies
- Church foyers
- Offices

Or give it as a gift for a

- Dorm room
- Office
- Teen's bedroom
- Home recreation room

Available at Christian bookstores everywhere, or use the handy "Shop-By-Mail" form below.

VISA and MASTERCARD accepted.

Please send me _____ poster(s) at $4.95 per poster.

HERE'S LIFE PUBLISHERS, INC.
P. O. Box 1576
San Bernardino, CA 92402-1576

NAME_____

ADDRESS_____

STATE_____ZIP_____

ORDER TOTAL $_____

SHIPPING and
HANDLING $_____
($1.00 for one poster,
$0.25 for each additional.
Do not exceed $4.00.)

APPLICABLE
SALES TAX (CA, 6%) $_____

TOTAL DUE $_____

PAYABLE IN US FUNDS.
(No cash orders accepted.)

☐ Payment (check or money order only) included
☐ Visa   ☐ Mastercard #_____

Expiration Date_____Signature_____

FOR FASTER SERVICE
CALL TOLL FREE: 1-800-950-4457   TCP 277-8

Your Christian bookstore should have these in stock. If not, use this "Shop-by-Mail" form.
PLEASE ALLOW 2 TO 4 WEEKS FOR DELIVERY.
PRICES SUBJECT TO CHANGE WITHOUT NOTICE.

KEEP UP WITH THE WAR IN FILM AND TELEVISION

Since American media will continue to be a primary battleground in the war between Judeo-Christian values and the values of the coming persecutors, it is especially important to be in touch with what is happening at the heart of media in Hollywood and New York. Mastermedia International, author Larry Poland's own organization, is committed to keeping you informed about spiritual and moral issues in media.

Write right now for your FREE subscription to **The Mediator!**

This informative, provocative and easy-to-read bi-monthly publication provides insights, critical concerns, evidences of God at work, stories of the spiritual war, and points for prayer and action.

It's yours for the asking!

— — — — — — — — — —

Please send me **The Mediator!**

_____
Name

_____
Street Address and Apartment Number

_____
City, State and Zip Code

Mail to:
Mastermedia International
409-E Palm Avenue
Redlands, CA 92373

An Inspiring "Do-It-Yourself" Bible Study

THE REVELATION

by Renowned Bible Teacher Irving Jensen

Dr. Irving Jensen's popular "Do-It-Yourself" inductive Bible study method helps make THE REVELATION come alive in both individual and group Bible study.

Your guide includes thought-provoking questions, suggestions for disucssion, and commentary on the biblical text.

Available at Christian bookstores everywhere, or use the handy "Shop-By-Mail" form below.

VISA and MASTERCARD accepted.

Please send me _____ copies of Irving Jensen's THE REVELATION at $7.95 per copy.

HERE'S LIFE PUBLISHERS, INC.
P. O. Box 1576
San Bernardino, CA 92402-1576

NAME_____

ADDRESS_____

STATE_____ZIP_____

ORDER TOTAL $_____

SHIPPING and
HANDLING $_____
($1.50 for one book,
$0.50 for each additional.
Do not exceed $4.00.)

APPLICABLE
SALES TAX (CA, 6%) $_____

TOTAL DUE $_____
PAYABLE IN US FUNDS.
(No cash orders accepted.)

☐ Payment (check or money order only) included
☐ Visa   ☐ Mastercard #_____

Expiration Date_____Signature_____

**FOR FASTER SERVICE
CALL TOLL FREE: 1-800-950-4457**   TCP 277-8

BUILDING BETTER FAMILIES

Practical Resources
to Strengthen Your Home

Quantity   Total

____ **FAMILY FITNESS FUN** *by Charles Kuntzleman.* $_____
Enjoy the sense of freedom that comes with feeling
healthier and more energetic by tapping into this
hassle-free handbook to a wholesome family lifestyle.
A book for the entire family with over 180 stimulating
strategies and activities for both parents and children.
ISBN 0-89840-279-4/$9.95

____ **HELPING YOUR KIDS HANDLE STRESS** *by H.* $_____
Norman Wright. Whether your child is a toddler or
teen, the author offers practical ways to spot a stress
problem, identify its source, and help your child learn
to cope with stress successfully.
ISBN 0-89840-271-9/$7.95

____ **PULLING WEEDS, PLANTING SEEDS: Grow-** $_____
ing Character in Your Life and Family *by Dennis*
Rainey. An inspiring collection of pointed reflections
on personal and family life with an abundance of practical insights for everyday living.
ISBN 0-89840-217-4/hardcover, $12.95

____ **MOM AND DAD DON'T LIVE TOGETHER** $_____
ANYMORE *by Gary and Angela Hunt.* Help and encouragement for youth and their parents who are
working through this confusing time. If a divorce has
happened in your family, your kids need to know that
they are not alone – or wierd – and that there is hope
for their future. ISBN 0-89840-199-2/$5.95

____ **TALKING WITH YOUR KIDS ABOUT LOVE,** $_____
SEX AND DATING *by Barry & Carol St. Clair.* The
topic which strikes fear in the heart of every parent!
Learn to resolve your fears and build an atmosphere
of love, trust and ongoing interaction with your kids
on these vital topics. ISBN 0-89840-241-7/$7.95

____ **THE DAD DIFFERENCE: Creating an Environ-** $_____
ment for Your Child's Sexual Wholeness *by Josh*
McDowell and Dr. Norm Wakefield. Sets the stage for
fathering that will dramatically improve parent/teen
relationships and reduce teen sexual excesses. Practical examples of role modeling and father/children activities. ISBN 0-89840-252-2/$8.95

(Continued on next page.)

Quantity		Total

DATING, LOVE, SEX GIFT SET, *Josh McDowell, Series Editor.* Making the right decisions for a great relationship . . . Series includes **DATING: PICKING (AND BEING) A WINNER, LOVE: MAKING IT LAST**, and **SEX: DESIRING THE BEST**. ISBN 0-89840-235-2/$19.95 — $____

PARENTING SOLO *by Dr. Emil Authelet.* Take the fear—and some of the frustration—out of single parenting. Helpful ideas for laying a strong biblical foundation, understanding your need for healing, and overcoming barriers that keep you and your children from growing and enjoying a fulfilling life. ISBN 0-89840-197-6/$7.95 — $____

IS THERE LIFE AFTER JOHNNY? Standing Strong Through Your Child's Rebellion *by Joy P. Gage.* A bold, biblical and personal look at emotional healing for the grieving parent of a wayward child. ISBN 0-89840-255-7/$7.95 — $____

Order Total $____

Indicate product(s) desired above. Fill out below.
Send to:

HERE'S LIFE PUBLISHERS, INC.
P. O. Box 1576
San Bernardino, CA 92402-1576

NAME_____

ADDRESS_____

STATE_____ZIP_____

☐ Payment (check or money order only) included
☐ Visa   ☐ Mastercard #_____

Expiration Date_____Signature_____

ORDER TOTAL $_____

SHIPPING and
HANDLING $_____
($1.50 for one book,
$0.50 for each additional.
Do not exceed $4.00.)

APPLICABLE
SALES TAX (CA, 6%) $_____

TOTAL DUE $_____

PAYABLE IN US FUNDS.
(No cash orders accepted.)

**FOR FASTER SERVICE
CALL TOLL FREE:
1-800-950-4457**

TCP 277-8

Your Christian bookstore should have these in stock. If not, use this "Shop-by-Mail" form.
PLEASE ALLOW 2 TO 4 WEEKS FOR DELIVERY.
PRICES SUBJECT TO CHANGE WITHOUT NOTICE.

HOLLYWOOD'S HISTORIC ATTACK ON CHRISTIANS

On August 12, 1988, Universal Pictures released **The Last Temptation of Christ,** a film which distorted the life and character of Jesus Christ, showing Him as lusting, bedeviled and in a sex act with Mary Magdalene.

The controversy surrounding the film, the American media's distortion of the facts of the protest and the advent of an unprecedented wave of media "Christian bashing" is the subject of Larry Poland's book . . .

The Last Temptation of Hollywood.

Larry Poland lived the story, and you won't want to miss his riveting 265-page story of an attempt to build bridges between Hollywood's biggest film studio and evangelical Christians. You'll learn how it ended in an international protest that changed the face of media.

Order your own personal copy!

— — — — — — — — — — —

Please send me _____ copies of **The Last Temptation of Hollywood** at $6.95 each. I enclose check or money order (no cash or credit cards please).

Order Total	$ _____
Shipping and Handling	$ __2.00__
Grand Total	$ _____

_____
Name

_____
Street Address and Apartment Number

_____
City, State and Zip Code

Mail to:
Mastermedia International
409-E Palm Avenue
Redlands, CA 92373

With its timely subject matter and group discussion guide, *The Coming Persecution* is an ideal book for Sunday school classes or group Bible studies.

For quantity purchases, contact your Christian bookseller or call TOLL FREE:

Here's Life Publishers
1-800-950-4457